WISING UP

WISING UP

RITUAL RESOURCES
FOR WOMEN OF FAITH
IN THEIR JOURNEY OF AGING

EDITED BY
KATHY BLACK AND
HEATHER MURRAY ELKINS

THE
PILGRIM
PRESS
Cleveland

The Pilgrim Press
700 Prospect Avenue
Cleveland, Ohio 44115-1100
thepilgrimpress.com

Printed in the United States of America on acid-free paper

09 08 07 06 05   5 4 3 2 1

Library of Congress Cataloging-in-Publication Data
    Wising up : ritual resources for women of faith in their journey of
aging / Kathy Black and Heather Murray Elkins, editors.
        p.   cm.
    ISBN 0-8298-1684-4 (alk. paper)
    1. Older women – Religious life. 2. Aging – Religious aspects. 3. Rites
and ceremonies. I. Black, Kathy, 1956- II. Elkins, Heather Murray.
BL625.7.W57 2005
264′.0084′6 – dc22
                                                            2005023267

Contents

Acknowledgments

This project began several years ago in the Feminist Studies in Liturgy group at the North American Academy of Liturgy. After three years of conversation on the topic of "Women, Aging, and Ritual," we offer our conclusions to you. Without these women scholars and teachers of liturgy, this project would not have been possible: Teresa Berger, Denise Dijk, Ruth Duck, Brigitte Enzner-Probst, June Goudey, Martha Whitmore Hickman, Martha Ann Kirk, Marcia McFee, Marjorie Procter-Smith, Susan Roll, Deborah Sokolove, Linda Vogel, Maggie Wenig, and Janet Walton. Thanks also to Susan Ray Beehler and Mary Elizabeth Mullino Moore, who contributed music and lyrics to our collection of rituals.

There are others, those named and unnamed, whose life stories are shared in this book: Among them are Norma Lee Barnhart, Angela Berlis, Gwyneth Black, Kay Bower, Lettie Frank, Flora Belle Hoyt, Clara Soto Ivey, Mary Kraus, Martha Lloyd, Elizabeth Heaton Mullino, Winnie Murray, Marjorie Suchocki, Jeanne Audrey Powers, Mary Shaw, Ada Sophie, Nancy Wilson, Pat Wilson, Adah, Ruth, Ursula, and the Presbyterian woman in Texas who shared the story of the ritual designed for her mother who needed to give up her car keys.

We are indebted to Kathy's research assistant, Jon Kwong, for his computer skill, and to Ulrike Guthrie from The Pilgrim Press for supporting us throughout the process.

Prelude

Heather and I have come together at my parents' cottage on a lake in the Pocono mountains of northeast Pennsylvania to put the finishing touches on this book. The cottage has been in my family for twenty-six years and thus is a place where two generations of family have gathered. It is a place filled with traditions and rituals: picking blueberries, deer spotting, skipping stones, sunset boat rides, tubing, eating peach cobbler, ice cream with pretzels, blueberry pancakes, and playing lots of card games. And yet, as my parents approach their eighties, it is time for them to seriously consider their transition into the fourth quarter of life. They are fortunate not to have had to deal with major aging issues so far. But now macular degeneration makes it too difficult for my mom to drive long distances, and my dad doesn't have the same kind of energy he used to have to make the drive and then do all the repairs that need to be done on a mountain cottage. And so my parents are choosing to pare back their lives, to make decisions while they can that will assist them in this journey of aging, such as not having to worry about a piece of property so far from their home. They have decided to sell this cottage and make other plans for family gatherings that are more manageable for this time in their lives.

The time is not yet right, but I hope that before my parents turn this cottage over to future new owners, our family will be able to come together for a time of thanksgiving for the multitude of memories and a leave-taking that honors our past with this cottage while at the same time affirming my parents' decision to move into this next stage of their life with wisdom and forethought. Their children (including myself) find it difficult to acknowledge this transition in our parents' lives, that they are getting older and should make the decisions that are right for them. One day in the future there will come a time when my parents will need to move out of their main home, where they have lived for over fifty years — the only home I ever knew growing up, the only home the grandchildren know as Mom-Mom and Poppy's. When that day comes, we will need to have another ritual, another time of naming the memories, affirming their decision, and then blessing their new space in the retirement home.

While it is difficult for me to leave this cottage knowing I may never be here again, such difficulty is exactly what this book is about. We wanted to provide rituals for women as they transition into the journey of aging, rituals that will name the grief, claim the ability to make choices and take control when possible, and affirm over and over that God is constantly present with us on the journey, guiding us until we finally rest in the arms of God.

Kathy Black

Blacks' Cottage
Lake Wallenpaupack
Pennsylvania

Introduction

We Are

We are women who study worship. We are feminists who put into practice what we teach in universities, seminaries, faith communities, and families. We're members of a guild, the North American Academy of Liturgy. At the start of each year we make an annual pilgrimage to our guild's meeting to share what we've learned from our work as worshiping women.

We are religiously diverse: Roman Catholic, Protestant, and Jewish, and regionally varied. We are — regrettably, from the point of view of this book — too uniform racially. We are all of European descent. We encourage our sisters from other cultures to take up the task of documenting rituals present in their

Feminist Studies of Liturgy Group, North American Academy of Liturgy. From left to right: Martha Ann Kirk, Linda Vogel, Brigitte Enzner-Probst, Marcia McFee, June Goudey, Susan Roll, Kathy Black, Heather Murray Elkins, Janet Walton.

Why This Book?

Liturgy or public worship that is inclusive of the old in explicit ways is rare. Retirements may be marked; deaths certainly are. In between, in those twenty-five or thirty years of human life, "there is a universe of differentiation that remains a cultural wasteland for each to calculate and navigate alone, without the aid of ritual, ceremony, or symbol."[1]

own contexts that have in the past and will continue in the future to support women in the process of aging. Our age range covers four decades. Several years ago, we took up the topic of "Women, Ritual, and Aging" in our Feminist Studies in Liturgy group. Our reasons were as varied as we are. We know we're aging, as women and as scholars in a field that is now reaching its "mature years." Some of us have retired, some are experiencing ill health, some are caring for parents in their older years, and others recognize that we are, at best, only temporarily able-bodied. We want to study new rituals that might deepen our experience of our own lives as women who are growing in wisdom, as well as getting older. We have a treasury of stories, some written and some oral, of the ways women mark, mourn, celebrate, and ritualize their aging.

We recognize that this is the first time in the history of the world that a significant number of women clergy are moving into the senior category. We want to take this into account both personally and professionally. Roman Catholic women who are members of religious orders have extensive experience in caring for and ritualizing the transitions experienced by the older members of their religious communities. Yet all of us are conscious of women, in faith communities and outside them, who are wishing there were rituals that would make the journey between growing up and growing old more meaningful and less stressful.

We are part of this generation that is witnessing aging in ourselves and our parents. We want to provide liturgical sustenance for both the positive and negative aspects of aging. Some of us are not married and don't have children we can depend on in our later years. Others do have children but don't want their children making choices for them or don't want to be a "burden" to their children. All of us recognize that there are few rituals available to mark the multitude of transitions and challenges that present themselves in aging — except for the final rite of passage: death. And even then, preparing one's own funeral or memorial rite is not often seen as an opportunity to prepare for dying or as a time to teach others the best of what we've learned.

We Want

We want to "wise up" before it's too late. We want to assist in creating our own community, a community of faith for the journey of aging. We want to be proactive; we want to anticipate the future in the midst of God's guiding presence and in the context of community rather than finding ourselves reactive to the often inevitable circumstances of our later years where so many find themselves isolated and without choice.

As we grow older, we want to have ritual resources available for those we love, for our parishioners, for our friends, and for ourselves. We want to name and claim God's presence with us throughout the various transitions that aging requires, including preparation for one's death. To these ends we've collected rituals that we and others have created and used over the years, and we have imagined some new ones that we know we'll need some day. We offer them to individuals and communities of faith who intend to grow in wisdom as well as grow older.

The face that time has marked looks not frail to us now — but wise. We understand that God knows those things only the passage of time can teach: that one can survive the loss of a love; that one can feel secure even in the midst of an ever-changing world; that there can be dignity in being alive even when every bone aches.[2]

—Rabbi Maggie Wenig

We Know

We know that many factors go into aging wisely and well. Poverty, lack of a supportive community, and limited mental capacity can hinder people's ability to live well regardless of their age. The multiple transitions and challenges of aging can be complicated even more by these other circumstances. While outside factors do impinge on our ability to age wisely and well, there are still many things that we can do to make this journey more meaningful and more spirit-filled.

To Lose One's Life Is to Gain It

Recognizing the losses in one's life and grieving these losses is crucial to being able to move on. In the Christian tradition we talk about losing one's life in order to gain it. During the aging process, a person often experiences many losses: loss of eyesight, loss of hearing, loss of ease in physical movement, loss of memory, loss of friends as they die, loss of confidence, loss of surety and stability, loss of independence, loss of income, loss of home if one needs to move to a retirement home or nursing home.

While these losses are natural in many cases, even expected, they are very difficult to take — especially when a cluster of such losses occurs within the span of a few years. Grieving these losses while recognizing they are a natural part of living is the first step in being able to move on with grace and anticipation, for as we lose something, it is often the case that we gain something: a new way of being in the world, new sensitivities, a new environment and group of friends, a sense of being at home with uncertainty and ambiguity, interdependence, a deeper spirituality.

Ritual can assist us to age wisely and celebrate what we have had, grieve what is lost, and imagine a new future for ourselves.

Change Happens

Whether we like it or not, we are constantly being changed. Some changes go unnoticed, some cause excitement for our future, and some evoke fear. Many changes in the journey of aging are viewed with a sense of impending dread or even panic. They are often unwelcome and unwanted changes. And yet every change in our lives poses alternative possibilities for our future. Aging wisely and well requires us to not stop at the crisis stage of change but to envision what opportunities are now possible for us, to imagine a future different from the past, adjusted by the present, but filled with hope.

Old age ain't no place for sissies.

—Bette Davis

The journey of aging requires many changes in one's life. For those who have enjoyed prolonged continuity and constancy in their lives, change is very difficult in aging. For those who, throughout their lives, have constantly adapted to change, this aspect of aging is easier to adjust to. For someone who has had good health all her life and has seldom gone to a doctor, a decline in health and scheduling one's life around doctors' appointments is disconcerting at best. For some, it triggers a sense of depression and foreboding. When a woman has been adapting to health issues most of her life, adapting to aging doesn't seem any different from the norm. For a person who has lived in the same house for forty-five years, moving into a retirement home is a far bigger change than for someone who has never spent more than eight years in the same place.

Change happens in many ways during the aging process: change in one's physical and mental abilities, change in one's community as some move away or die, change in one's habits of being (needing to remember to take medicine or adjusting to living alone), change in the thoughts that preoccupy one's mind (economic worries, memory loss, inevitable death). There can be greater changes as well: change in status from being married to being a widow; change in the way one views oneself (from being partnered to being single); change in the way one gets around (with the assistance of a cane or walker or wheelchair); change in how one "does errands" (by bus or by depending on a friend) when one is no longer able to drive.

As we imagine possibilities in the midst of the multitude of changes in our lives, aging wisely and well also means accepting things that can't be changed. Some people spend their lives denying anything is wrong with them (they don't have a hearing loss) or they spend all their time and money seeking youthfulness, or they fall into despair. Part of aging well is being able to accept those things that cannot be changed, to learn to live with our limitations and yet not be controlled by them. We believe it is possible to manage our limitations without letting the limitations become the whole of who we are.

Ritual can help us recognize what can't be changed. And when change is required, ritual can assist us in naming the crisis, venting our anger and frustration at the need to change, acknowledging our tendency to resist change, and yet guide us into the possible opportunities that await us on the journey.

Who We Are Is More Than What We Do

American society places great value on doing. One of the first questions we ask of a new person we meet is "What do you do?" We value work, contributing to society, activity. After a certain age (usually around age eighteen) one is expected to "do." Those who don't have a job, those who aren't active, those who lie around all day, society judges as lazy, incompetent, shiftless, worthless, a drain on society. While society may ease up on those expectations for persons over sixty-five (of retirement age, having worked all their lives), many people over seventy have been taught that to be of value is to be able to "do"; to have a meaningful life means being able to "do." Therefore in the journey of aging, when we are not able to "do" in the same way as we could before, we begin to devalue ourselves, to see ourselves as burdens, to believe that we are worthless. We have lost the biblical concept that we are valued as children of God because of who we *are*, not because of what we can *do*.

To age wisely and well means to be able to value who we are, to value being as much as, if not more than, doing. Who we are — our mind, our spirit, our sense of humor, our personality — has much to offer the world regardless of what we can or cannot do.

For many of us, this notion of doing versus being translates into "giving" and "receiving." Women have been taught all their lives to give to others. We are taught to believe that it is "more blessed to give than to receive." And yet, in the journey of aging, women are not always as able to give — to do things for their children, their church, their friends, their community. In the journey of aging, there may very well come a time when we have to cultivate the talent of receiving and learn how to receive as graciously as we have given all our lives.

*O God . . . When the signs of age begin to mark my body
(and still more when they touch my mind); when the ill
that is to diminish me or carry me off strikes from without
or is born within me; when the painful moment comes
in which I suddenly awaken to the fact that I am ill or
growing old; and above all at that last moment when I
feel I am losing hold of myself and am absolutely passive
within the hands of the great unknown forces that have
formed me; in all those dark moments, O God, grant that
I may understand that it is you (provided only my faith
is strong enough) who are painfully parting the fibres of
my being in order to penetrate to the very marrow of my
substance and bear me away within yourself.*[3]

*Ritual can reclaim our belief that we are valued as children
of God, not because of what we do but because of who we
are. Rituals done for our benefit can help us cultivate the
blessed practice of receiving as graciously as we have given.*

Interdependence Is Not a Dirty Word

For those who have been independent all their lives, being dependent on anything or anyone is very difficult to take. Any
form of dependency makes one feel somehow less a person. It's
okay to depend on eyeglasses or contact lenses because that is
acceptable at any age in this society. It's acceptable to take vita-
mins every day of one's life. But when one is dependent upon
prescription medicine or has to get bifocals or a hearing aid or
a cane or walker, then suddenly it is a different matter. Any
dependency is a sign of our mortality, of our aging, and many
of us resist it, especially if it is visible enough that other people
will know we are dependent upon a device and therefore not
"capable" anymore.

When we have to depend on another person — family member, friend, paid caregiver — the sense of dependency, the loss of dignity and personhood, can be even greater. We don't want to be a burden on anyone to drive us to the grocery store, bank, or church. When one has to be fed, clothed, bathed, or helped to the bathroom, all modesty is gone, and it feels as if one's dignity has been violated. Dependency can make us feel "child-like," and we can lose our sense of self.

The value our society has placed on independence, doing for oneself, is deeply embedded in our psyches. To age wisely and well, however, we have to be able to rethink notions of dependency and independency and acknowledge that we are all interdependent. Our world is intricately related. We are a web of living creatures. Nothing stands totally independent of another.

In the Christian tradition, this community of interdependence is underscored in 1 Corinthians 12:14–26, where we are reminded that the body consists of many members and just because we are not an important part of the body doesn't mean we don't belong to the body. All are needed to make the body work. At different points in our lives we may be more dependent on others, but it doesn't mean that we don't also give to others. There is an interdependency that is woven into the fabric of relationality. "If one member suffers, all suffer together with it; if one member is honored, all rejoice together with it" (v. 26). We are all interconnected.

This apprehension of dependency on things or dependency on people in the later years of life can lead to isolation. People who can't hear decide not to go to church or out to restaurants or concerts or parties. Those who can't walk well give up going to museums or shopping for their grandchildren. People who are dependent on adult diapers don't want to be too far away from home. People who need help being fed or clothed find going out too much trouble. It is easier to stay home, alone. Easier, perhaps, but it often leads to isolation, loneliness, and depression. Part of interdependency is that we continue to be a part of community. That community may be only a couple of people, but community is crucial to one's well-being at any age. Maintaining community in our later years when we may become dependent on things or people requires effort and intentionality and courage.

As we attempt to age with dignity and grace, it is important to acknowledge that there will probably come a time for each of us when being dependent on things or people is necessary and all right. We realize that independence is an illusion. In reality we are interdependent, interconnected creatures among whom there is a constant give and take.

Ritual can reaffirm our interdependence upon God and one another and enable us to maintain our value (however changing that may be) in the communities of which we are a part.

How Old Is Old?

As we began our work on this book, one of our first questions was: "How old is old?" When does aging begin? One of our youngest members (in her forties) has had to buy a walker already. She was faced with issues of physical limitation, dependency, adaptation, giving up a sense of modesty when others had to take care of her, the stares of others, and facing mortality at an earlier age than most of us experience. Another among us (in her fifties), even though she herself was in good health, felt as if she was already "old" because she had outlived her mother, who died at the age of forty-one. One of us is over seventy and is rightly offended when less than perfect strangers on elevators tell their children to "let the old people get out first." Two of us with grandmothers who lived over a century think middle age starts at sixty.

In many ways "aging" is a state of mind. For some, aging begins when we start to consider our lives in terms of how much is left rather than how far we've come. Though the Bureau of Census of the United States defines old age as being sixty-five years old and more,[4] "old" is not really about chronological age but is self-defined. We all know folk who are "too old too soon" and those who are "young at heart" way beyond their years.

You know you're old when your children join the AARP.

— Pat Wilson

Aging is often self-defined by some health crisis in a person's life: a heart attack, high blood pressure, a stroke, a knee replacement, diagnosis of cancer, loss of hearing, significant memory loss. When our physical being and mental capacities are operating as usual, people don't think about aging in the same way. They don't consider themselves "old" or "elderly" regardless of their age. But when there is some crisis in one's physical or mental condition, aging becomes a present reality no matter what one's age.

A person who has a heart attack at age forty-two is faced with her mortality and knows the experiential reality of aging: loss, grief, adaptation, change. Society tends to associate life's reality with one's physical condition because we value what people can do, not who they are. So when one's physical body is limited in some way, it tends to define the whole of the person. But aging does not have to be totally defined by lack of physical or mental ability. Some people do their best work in their later years, and for others it is a time not for work but for being the best they can be.

One of the problems is that the assumed model for aging is the "Rise-Peak-Decline" model (sometimes called the low-high-low model). We assume there is a peak somewhere in midlife and it is all downhill from there on. But this "Rise-Peak-Decline" way of viewing our lives does not have to be the dominant metaphor. The "decline" aspect of this model (often referred to as the "third stage of life") implies that it is inevitable and we have no say in the matter.[5] We should just sit back and let the rest of life happen to us. Yet some experts in gerontology[6] argue that this model is an illusion; that we should re-envision life as a constant "upward curve."

> *Wising up can be a time in which we live in the midst of rich experiential knowledge, inspired wisdom, deep spirituality, and in which we enjoy both long-term and new relationships. We want to and know we can prepare to look forward with joy and anticipation to the "climax of our life's journey."*[7]

Why Women Only?

Obviously the rituals offered in this book will be important for men as well, but studies show that there is a "feminization of death" in our culture.[8] It is a sad statistic that men die younger, and it means that the vast majority of our seniors are women. Of the 35 million persons over the age of sixty-five in the 2000 U.S. census data, 14.4 million were men and 20.6 million were women. Beyond seventy-five and beyond eighty-five years of age, the ratio of women to men is even greater. While one might have assumed that with more women taking on the stresses of full-time work, with modern technology and medical advances, this ratio would even out or at least decrease, this is not the case. The ratio of women to men has increased in all the age groupings over sixty-five since the 1990 census. These statistics correlate to the status of those widowed. Fifty-one percent of women over the age of sixty-five are widowed compared to only 13 percent of men.[9] And the "mean duration of widowed life is approximately fourteen years for women and seven years for men." Men die sooner after their wives die than women do after their husbands die.[10] For these reasons, women are the inheritors and inhabitants of the later years of life.

Because women live longer, many have developed communities among themselves. Widows have found unstructured but highly effective ways of adapting and gathering around newly widowed women to help them through grief and transition. Women help other women know when they should give up driving. They gather over lunch or around the kitchen table and support one another through the difficult times. They bring food, send cards, drive one another to doctors' appointments. Women adopt new skills and adapt old ways, adjusting to new circumstances, persevering throughout the hard times and struggles. This adaptation has been a normal part of life, and it is often this ability to adapt well and to live with ambiguity that is necessary for the journey of aging.

What's to Follow?

We've divided the book into four chapters that deal with various issues of aging. Within each chapter are multiple rituals. We begin with a contemporary revision of Psalm 71 that names God's presence throughout the aging process.

The first chapter then deals with the issue of "Practicing Partnership" — with things, with an individual, with a community. Our first ritual, "Partnering with Things," is for a person who buys a walker and begins the journey of a partnership with this walker. In the aging process, there often comes a time when a person depends on things — a pacemaker, a hearing aid, a cane, or a wheelchair. We have a tendency to conceive of these items as alien to our body. Because they are often symbols of a body that is degenerating or visibly aging, they are often unwanted but "necessary evils." We want to re-imagine our relationship with these "things" as a partnership, a collaboration. We want to adopt them, adapt to them, incorporate them because they are a part of us. The second ritual, "Life Partners," is a covenant ceremony between two individuals who commit themselves to be partners to each other for life but choose not to marry. Among our older population, there are more and more who want to join their lives together in the presence of God and their family and friends but do not want the legal bond of marriage for tax purposes and for inheritance reasons. The third ritual in this chapter is called "Partnering with Community" and is about partnering with a community. A woman is at the point where it is unsafe for her to continue to drive. Her community gathers to recall the role she played in their busy lives driving them to and fro and covenants with her to be there for her in the way she was for them. We close this chapter with a hymn by Ruth Duck, who affirms that God is our partner even in the midst of pain.

The second chapter, "Being Changed," deals with the reality of change and transitions in our lives. We look in the mirror and wonder how we came to look like this. Bodies change; minds become forgetful. For some it is the physical body that feels strange — we can't hear very well anymore, can't walk like we used to. For others it is the mental/memory part of one's life that feels strange and alien. Changes happen as an integral part of aging. In some instances the change we mourn may yield other possibilities or benefits. In other situations, however, the change can be devastating. Rituals in this chapter include "Change of Life: A Flash of Insight" for women experiencing menopause; "Celebrating Change: Croning," which honors a woman's sixtieth birthday; and "Changing Roles: Becoming Orphaned," which reflects one's transition to becoming the oldest generation in the family, the new matriarch. Our last ritual in this chapter is entitled "Changing Self: Growing Stranger." It addresses those who experience memory loss and find they are becoming strangers to themselves and to others. Ruth Duck's hymn "When Earth Is Changed" reflects on catastrophe, illness, death, and suffering and yet claims God's sheltering presence through it all.

The third chapter focuses on "Making Choices." When change happens, there are always choices to be made. Not making a choice is its own choice. Short story writer Martha Hickman begins this chapter with "The Woman Who Wouldn't Grow Old." "To Dye or Not to Dye" follows and deals with the choices women make about dying their hair and wearing hats. The ritual "More Blessed to Receive" tells the story of a missionary woman who strongly believed it was more blessed to give than to receive. And yet, knowing she had only a short time to live, she chose to allow the community to give to her, and she graciously received their thanksgivings and blessings. "Radical Choice" is a ritual designed by a community for a woman who chose to have radical surgery to have both breasts removed because of cancer. In "The Willing of Things," a woman shares her plans for the choices she has made to "will" her life's work, her personal papers, her possessions, her finances, and eventually her body to others. The last ritual in this chapter is "Creating Community: Rituals of Recognition," which offers rituals that create new communities of nurture and support for women who by choice or by circumstance live together in community in the last season of their lives.

The last chapter is entitled "Going Home" and includes a wide diversity of rituals that help prepare for the inevitable — death. It begins with a song by Susan Beehler called "Let Me Go Home." It is the song of a woman who has had a long and wonderful life yet has come to the place where she wants to "go home" and is confident that God will guide her there. The first ritual in this chapter, "A Serendipitous Dance of Death," tells the story of a woman from our group who danced at her mother's funeral service, celebrating not only her life but her being welcomed in death into the arms of God. "A Country Way of Dying" names the importance of recording the distinct and diverse traditions of holy dying within oral communities such as those in Appalachia. "Now I Lay Me Down to Sleep" tells the story of a woman who was diagnosed with a degenerative terminal illness. The woman asked her pastor to design a ritual that would help her "pass over" when she decided the time was right. "Daybreak" is a hymn written by Mary Elizabeth Mullino Moore for her mother's funeral. "Facing Finitude: Between 'Now' and 'the Hour of Our Death'" is an essay that ends with a poem/prayer asking God's Holy Wisdom and Vibrant Presence to uphold us as we face our own aging process and cross over into the arms of God.

While each ritual is designed differently, when possible we have included a narrative of the woman involved, the context, and a little of her story that led to the ritual. We then present the ritual itself. Following each ritual are some questions and suggestions to help you consider how to adapt this ritual for your specific needs. Wisdom sayings, quotations, poems, and prayers are interspersed throughout to offer alternative perspectives on "Wising Up." As you will see, the rituals include different components and have different structures. Feminist ritual is multifaceted just as we are a diverse group of women. There is no one right way to do ritual. Not only are the rituals diverse in content and structure, but the theology expressed in each ritual is also distinctive and reflective of that woman's or community's theological stance.

We encourage you to use these rituals to spark your own imagination. You have our permission to use them "as is" if you wish. But since they were designed for a specific person in a specific time and place, we encourage you to use these rituals as foundations or templates for your own creations. Adapt, edit, add to, or omit that which doesn't work for your context. Or start from scratch. Join with the Creator in the joy of creating a ritual for another woman that helps her name the struggle, claim God's presence, and envision her place in this journey of aging.

Getting Started

For those of you who don't have experience in designing rituals, here are a few questions and guidelines for developing rituals in general. More specific suggestions are provided at the end of each ritual.

Who: Who is the person the ritual will be designed for? Is it yourself, someone you love, a family member, a member of the congregation? Who else will be invited to participate in this ritual? A woman had a private ritual with her mom when it was time for her mom to give up her driver's license. A congregation invited anyone who wanted to come to celebrate the life of an active member who was dying of cancer, and over a hundred people showed up. Rituals can be designed for any number of people. Who do you anticipate will come to this ritual?

What: What is the issue of aging, the transition into a new phase of one's life that is being marked, the specific occasion for this ritual? Is this to be a ritual of healing after the death of a spouse or a ritual of leave-taking and blessing a new environment as a woman leaves her home and moves to a retirement community? Is it a ritual of adjustment and adaptation as the woman partners with a hearing aid or eye patch, a cane or wheelchair, another person who is to provide attendant care? Is it a ritual of celebration as one turns sixty or seventy or eighty or even a hundred years of age? Is it a ritual of mourning over the loss of a person, the loss or a particular function of the body or mind, or the loss of the ability to bear children anymore? Is it a welcoming ritual as widows embrace a newly widowed woman into their circle of community? Is it a ritual that begins to name and prepare for the inescapable reality of death? What kind of ritual is needed for this particular person at this time in her life?

Where: Where will the ritual take place? The church, someone's home, outside in a park? Will it happen by the altar, around a kitchen or dining room table, or surrounded by the beauty of nature?

When: When is the appropriate day and time?

How: How will this ritual unfold? Who will design the ritual? Who should be involved in the planning?

Components: Rituals can include a variety of components. Decide which elements work best for your context:

Prayers
   • taken from various resources
   • said extemporaneously
   • written for the occasion

Poetry
   • taken from various resources
   • written for the occasion

Scripture Texts
   • appropriate for the occasion
   • favorite passages of the woman

Responsive Readings
   • readings where there is a leader and a response from the others gathered; the response may vary each time or it may be repetitive, as in a litany

Quotations
   • from historical or contemporary folk
   • from books, movies, plays

Music
   • instrumental music played live or on a tape or CD
   • music sung by a soloist
   • music sung by all gathered

Symbols

- cloths (on the altar or coffee table or kitchen table) — white linens, family quilts, cloths of particular cultures, scarves, red-checkered plastic picnic cloths
- oil for anointing, for healing, or for blessing
- colors (one ritual on menopause calls for blues and greens — cool and calming colors — to counteract the hot flashes that spark bright reds and oranges)
- symbols of the earth: water, rocks, shells, flowers
- symbols of our daily lives: buttons, keys, balloons

Visuals

- slides or video of the person past and present
- slides or video of the people in her life
- slides or video of her favorite places

Design: How does one begin a ritual or end a ritual? What is the movement or development so that it flows throughout? Consider a basic structure:

Gathering

- Provide music for meditation or to set the tone.
- Serve food if appropriate.
- Ask people to read certain parts of the ritual.

Beginning

- Welcome the people gathered.
- Name the reason for the occasion in some sort of introduction.
- Talk about the issue of aging being faced: marking the transition, wanting to provide love and support for the person, claiming God's presence on the journey.
- Identify any symbols present — cloths, candles, rocks, car keys, walker.

Middle

- Provide an opportunity for the woman and those gathered to name the fears and uncertainties of the

present and the future, acknowledge the grief over
the losses, celebrate the past, offer words of hope
and support for the woman's future.
* Include a prayer, a poem, a song, a scripture reading,
or a contemporary reading.

Ending
* Bless the woman and the community gathered.
* Express a commitment or covenant with the woman
(for example, if she has just given up her car keys,
a covenant with her to drive her to the grocery store,
church, etc.).
* Claim God's presence in the midst of transition and
uncertainty.
* Close with a prayer or song or reading.
* Send the community forth to trust God and be of service
to one another and to the world.

As the chapters and rituals dealing with the various issues of
aging unfold in this book, we offer more specific questions and
suggestions to guide you in adapting these rituals or creating
your own for your particular context. We have also provided
an appendix (page 179) that lists more resources that deal
specifically with ritual design.

Our hope is that faith communities will embrace the women
among them who are living through the transitions of aging,
provide supportive communities where rituals can help facili-
tate the challenges of aging, and remind us all that God goes
with us on this journey of life and that when life's journey ends,
God is present with us in whatever lies ahead.

Psalm 71

God,
you have been my vision and my hope
since the very beginnings of my life.
In my mother's womb, you were with me.
You were the midwife who eased me into this world,
You the giver of the gift of life.
You let me flourish, bloom, and ripen.
My praise rises towards you continually
like whiffs of perfume from my body.
In you I trust all the days of my life
my refuge, my shelter, my home.

Now, in the middle of my life,
I look both back and to the future.
Do not forsake me as I grow old,
as my strength begins to lessen.

Those who always envied me your gifts of energy and power
will laugh at me:
You are beginning to look really old!
And they will think:
She is fair game now,
no divine power can save her from old age.

God, shield me
from those who consider me senile and useless.
Let them see your strength and power
even in my frailty and weakness.
Confound those who idolize youth

with your love for both young and old.
Confuse them with your own repeated trust in old women,
women like Sarah, Hannah, and Elizabeth,
whom you called to birth hope in old age.

Since my youth you have taught me
to discern your wisdom and presence in all
and to walk in your strength.
Do not leave me
as I turn old and gray,
as my body begins to show signs of weakness and frailty.
Let women friends be at my side
who want to age with me:
who want to become old and wise,
old and young at heart,
old and rich in lived life.

And at the very end of my life
be midwife for me once more.

Ease me out of this world
back into your own womb.
Until that precious hour
my mouth will speak of your justice and power
every day of my life.
I will glorify your faithfulness with my lute.
I will gladly sing your praise with full lungs,
God of my youth and of my old age.
To my children and my children's children
I will speak of your amazing power
which you pour out on all ages.[11]

Chapter One

Practicing Partnership

Wising up is a hands-on, not a hands-off process for women. In this opening chapter we offer the witness and the work of women who practice laying hands on creation in the holy work of human blessing. We believe that wisdom consists in learning to partner in community and communion with God. Because this is a lifelong lesson, it requires practice. We practice — that is, we explore how to carry out, to apply, to do or perform often, to work at repeatedly — so as to become proficient with the living essence of our lives. We grow wiser about the burdens we must learn to live with and which restrictions we can cheerfully toss in the trash. We learn to trust the ways we are physically and socially linked together. We practice letting go and holding on. We trust that we are not alone. We partner with one another, with God, and with the stuff of this material world.

Partnering with Things

KATHY BLACK

Aging came very early for me. By the time I was thirty-nine, I was having difficulty standing for any length of time, I couldn't walk for more than a block or two, I was dizzy a lot, going up stairs was extremely difficult, and I had spells where I would become totally paralyzed. I could hear and feel, but I couldn't move any muscle, open my eyes, speak, or control my breathing. They lasted only fifteen minutes to an hour, but it would take me another couple of hours to recuperate. These spells could be triggered by heat, standing, walking, bending over, pain. I had a battery of tests at various hospitals to no avail. I was raised on a toxic waste dump — the no. 1 Superfund site on the federal government's EPA list in 1982. Who knows what the exposure to a combination of twenty-one highly toxic substances could do to one's body? The advice: cope and manage. So I did. I learned how to monitor my every move to avoid risky behaviors. I made all decisions based on how they would affect my body. I gave up all sense of modesty since people were often carrying me or undressing me to put me in bed.

When I wasn't at work, I started to stay home more and more. It's true that I needed a lot of "down" time, regular rest, and a consistent eating schedule, but I was also staying home because I couldn't "manage." I stopped going to the mall to shop for birthday or Christmas presents. I stopped going to museums or botanical gardens because I couldn't walk very far. Many movie theaters required walking up steps to get far enough away from the screen so that the motion in the movie didn't make me dizzy and nauseous. Flying, especially by myself, was becoming almost impossible.

I didn't want to be a burden on anyone. I certainly didn't want to have a spell at a dinner party and disrupt everything. So it was easier to stay home. After a while, it feels as if people stop inviting you to join them because they know it "will be too much for you" or "it might be too risky." I became more and more isolated.

I still have a full deck; I just shuffle slower now.

—Anonymous

I began to realize that my condition could take over my life if I didn't do something about it. Since part of coping and managing is being creative, I tried to figure out what I could partner with that would allow me to stay more active and feel less isolated. I decided I needed a movable seat. I needed to be able to sit when I got dizzy or hot or felt a spell coming on. And if that seat had wheels and could move from painting to painting in an art gallery or from plant to plant in a botanical garden or from shirt to pants in a clothing store, then all the better. If it could also be used as a wheelchair so someone could push me after a spell, then the one device could function on multiple levels. It needed to fold up so I could put it in the trunk of my car and be light enough for me to handle when I was weak.

Once I decided what I needed, it took a long time to find it. The walker I finally bought has four wheels, bicycle brakes that can lock in place, a seat, a flexible back rest, and a removable wire basket. If I sit on it one way, I can steer it backwards. If I sit on it facing the other way, it can be used as a wheelchair and someone can push me. The flexible back rest allows one to sit facing either way.

It needed some adjustments and personal touches. It needed to be taller (the manufacturers assume these are made for short people — mostly women — who are shrinking or slumped over), the walker wouldn't fold up with the basket attached, there was no place for a water bottle, etc. So I set about customizing it for my own purposes.

The reactions of my friends and family varied. Some bemoaned the fact that my health had gotten to this point and I was so young: "Too bad..." "So sorry..." "Well, if you have to, you have to..." "What a shame." This "thing" would be a sign to the world of my degeneration. It would be an alien object symbolizing decline, loss of independence, loss of capability. One of my closest friends thought it was a huge mistake. She was sure that if I got the walker, I would stop using my muscles and they would atrophy and I would get worse and worse. It would be downhill from here on. I would buy into "defeat" in some way and let my health problems control me.

But my health problems were already controlling me. My schedule outside of work was dictated by doctors' appointments. My decisions were all being made in terms of the risk to my health. My body, what it could and could not handle, determined just about everything in my life. And I knew that if I didn't do something about it, I would become more and more isolated.

It was easy to buy into society's stereotypes. I was so young to have a walker. It was hard to deal with the stares, hard to convince people at the airline counters that it really was my walker and not a stroller for a baby, hard to explain to people why I needed it some times but not others. It was expected that I would resist getting a walker at my age. It was assumed that it would be an alien "thing," an "evil" — a necessary evil, but still a negative.

It took me a while to shift my thinking in relationship to my walker: to see it as a partner rather than alien to me, to lay hands on it and bless it for all it did for me rather than resist it or want to get rid of it as soon as possible.

In reality, the walker was a marvelous partner in freedom for me. Without the walker these past ten years, I could never have done all the things I have. I couldn't have managed the international travel I've done, the museums I've visited, shopping for the right birthday presents for my nieces. I could never have taken my nephew to Disneyland or Legoland. My walker has been my constant companion from Australia to Europe to the Yucatan Peninsula and all over the United States. "She" has held the weight of my computer and everything else I've needed to carry. "She" pulls my suitcase behind her with the help of a bungee cord. "She" offers me a seat wherever I am, two arms to lean on when I'm wobbly, and provides a safe, comforting presence when I am alone and feeling lousy. "She" has been a true partner throughout this part of my life.

Over time, some friends came to appreciate the benefits of my walker. They liked traveling with me because we were able to pre-board and not stand in the long lines, having plenty of time and space to stow carry-on luggage. They also liked having me along on trips to Disneyland since having the walker gained us entrance to the rides through the back door without waiting in the lines to go through the front entrance.

There are still rocky times. Not everything is accessible, and lifting the walker up curbs or steps is harder than not having a walker with me at all. Roads of dirt, sand, or rock make pushing the walker very difficult and drains energy from me that the walker is supposed to be helping to save. The feeling of security I gained from the walker has tricked me into traveling to unknown territories that were not accessible with a walker and has often created more problems.

Many church sanctuaries also are not designed to allow people to keep their walkers with them. So the usher brings the walker back to the narthex so that it is not a fire hazard in the aisle. But then one has to wait for everyone to exit and the usher to bring the walker back before one can leave. It would be so much better if churches would cut off the ends of several pews to allow people with walkers and persons using wheelchairs to be present in the sanctuary with their "partner" — whatever device they need. Physical access as well as attitudinal and theological access need to be addressed by the church.

At the time I bought the walker, I didn't have a ritual to help me "partner" with my walker. A good friend who was visiting from the East Coast shopped for the walker with me and helped me customize it for my needs. We designed and sewed a cloth basket so that I could keep things in the basket while it was folded up. We raised the handles so I didn't have to bend over so much to use it, and we tried to figure out a way to attach a holder for a water bottle (still no success with that one!).

Here are some suggestions for a ritual that would have helped make the transition easier for me.

Ritual for Partnering with Things

Who to Invite: I would invite close friends, family in the area, a few friends from church, a few friends from work. I wouldn't want the group too large — maybe ten or twelve.

Where: I don't think it matters where the ritual would take place. It could be held in my home or the home of a friend or at the church in a parlor or a "nice looking" classroom. I would want the people gathered to be sitting in some sort of a circle.

Symbol: The walker would be the primary symbol for the ritual, a part of the circle.

Shared Story or Shared Proclamation: I would want to acknowledge the reality of the situation, name the loss, let others name their fears, reclaim God's promise of valuing us as God's beloved not by what we can or cannot do, imagine new possibilities by partnering with the walker, and celebrate God's continuing presence on this new stage of life's journey.

Symbolic Action: We would lay hands on the walker and bless it as a new partner in life.

Gathering *(words offered by one in the group)*

We gather to welcome a new partner into the life of Kathy and into the life of this community. We gather to grieve the losses, name our fears, claim the hope of a new future, and celebrate God's presence with us on the various twists and turns of life.

A walker in our society symbolizes aging, dependency, degeneration, lack of ability, needing assistance. It proclaims to the world that one can no longer do for oneself. To varying degrees we've all bought into this image of the walker. For those who get one, it is often perceived as a necessary evil.

For the person getting the walker there are always questions: Does it symbolize that I have given up the struggle to get better? Is there something more I can do that would make me strong enough that I wouldn't need the walker? Have I given in? Will life be downhill from here on out? Will it make me worse or better? How will people treat me differently?

Friends and family have the same questions and even more. There may be underlying fears about one's own vulnerability, one's own prejudices about people who use walkers or wheelchairs. This is all quite natural. We've been conditioned by society's fears of ill health, aging, and mortality.

Concerns of the Community *(addressed to the community gathered, offered by anyone in the group)*

It's time for truth and honesty. What concerns and fears do you bring to this occasion? What cautions and hesitations linger? *(for example: you haven't done enough to seek a "cure"; it will make your muscles atrophy; you've given up in defeat, etc.).*

Naming the Losses *(addressed to Kathy)*

What losses will you grieve? What fears remain?

Prayer

Gracious God, who goes with us on every step of our journey, be with us now as we grieve the loss of easy movement, being able to come and go as we pleased, a life uncontrolled by concern for health and safety. Enable us to experience your presence in the difficult transitions of life, drawing on your comfort and strength. Now inspire our imaginations for new possibilities, new hopes, new blessings that can come from Kathy partnering with this walker. Amen.

Hopes of the Community

What hopes do you have for this partnership? What will Kathy be able to do with the walker that was difficult or not possible before? *(for example, hopes that Kathy can visit museums again, go shopping, enjoy whatever activities she has given up lately, become a part of the community again).*

Laying on of Hands

Bring the walker into the center of the circle. Everyone gathers around and lays a hand on the walker. A representative of the gathered community offers these words:

We bless this walker as a new partner for Kathy. Provide her security when she is unsteady, rest when she can't stand, a place to hold her heavy burdens. May your presence offer Kathy a new freedom to go places, see new things, and continue her participation in the various communities of which she is a part.

Kathy: I welcome this walker as a new partner, a wonderful companion to go with me through the next stage of my life.

Prayer

Loving God, go with each one of us through the joys and challenges of life. Be our constant guide and companion as we seek to support one another and be servants in your world. Amen.

Benediction Song

Blessing

Susan R. Beehler

...words on the end of a letter from Rev. Mary Kraus

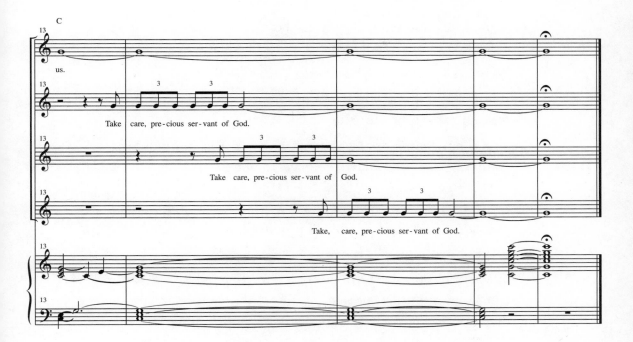

After the ritual, those gathered may help customize the walker to give it personal touches and adjust it to Kathy's needs. Then eat and celebrate!

Adaptability

This ritual can be adapted to a variety of contexts.

Who is the person that needs to partner with a "thing"? Is it a family member, a friend, several within a women's group at church?

What is the "thing" that will be the new partner? It may be a walker or it may be a hearing aid, a cane, a wheelchair, a prosthesis, even another person — a stranger who is providing attendant care.

When and *Where* will this ritual take place? In someone's home on a weekday evening, a Saturday morning, or Sunday afternoon? Or might it take place in church during a Sunday night "healing" service where there is a "blessing of the assistive devices" that contribute to our healing?

Who will be invited to the ritual?

Symbol: The "thing" that will be the new partner should be the central symbol for the ritual.

Fears: What fears (of the individual or of the individual's community) accompany the need to get the assistive device in the first place?

Hopes: What hopes for the future are imbedded in this assistive device for greater freedom in hearing or getting around or caring for oneself?

Prayers: What do we need from God at this time of transition? Is it God's comfort, presence, and guidance for this journey that are needed? Or are we asking God for patience, the ability to adapt, the letting go of ego and stubbornness?

Readings: What readings from scripture or poetry or other sources might be helpful for the occasion?

Songs: What songs might inspire hope for the future and companionship along the way?

Symbolic Action: Will there be some sort of symbolic action that will bless the assistive device (or person), to claim its presence as a partner rather than a "necessary evil"?

Life Partners

HEATHER MURRAY ELKINS

She had just turned eighty and was described as "elegant" by friends and strangers. Her handmade hats were her trademark. He'd been a shy man for over seventy years, going bald with good grace, a handy man who knew what to do with dysfunctional toasters and plumbing. She was a longtime widow. He'd lost his wife five years ago. If you asked one to an event, you'd better ask them both. They sat together in the same pew, went out to eat, drove together for groceries and to the doctors. They were a couple, not in name but in practice.

Why didn't they marry? Many in the congregation knew their delicate balance of limited pensions and memory-filled homes. There were adult children who openly resisted. There was the question of legal rights to determine what medical solutions were offered when the time came. They had not been partners for life, but they did want to be together as long as life permitted with the blessing of their community in Christ.

What makes a union of two people in the presence of God acceptable to a faith community? Does a service of Christian partnering require legal sanction or a presiding minister? Should making a promise to care for each other in Christ's name always require paperwork?

These questions tend to tie politics and religion into legal knots. The property rights as well as the proper recognition and support of children of a union are essential aspects of a marriage contract. For Christians, these social and economic commitments are interpreted through the scriptural and theological understanding of Christ's relationship to the church as symbolized by Jesus' presence at a wedding. Although marriage eventually came to be interpreted as one of the seven sacraments in some traditions, there was no uniform requirement for church-recognized marriages until the Council of Trent (1545–63). Government registration of marriages wasn't a widespread practice until the end of the eighteenth century.

In the *Decree for the Armenians,* marriage is characterized by: "first, the begetting of children and their bringing up in the worship of the Lord; secondly, the fidelity that husband and wife should each maintain toward the other; thirdly, the indissoluble character of marriage, for this typifies the indissoluble union of Christ and the Church."[12]

The first purpose of marriage, the begetting and raising of children, was not applicable to this situation, and the third reason, the indissoluble character of marriage, has been steadily dissolving as a cultural norm with too few theologically sound alternatives. What might the second reason offer for interpreting the need for a life ritual for partnership when a legally recognized marriage isn't an option?

There is growing evidence that older adults who describe themselves as religious or spiritual elders are forming partnerships that are not legally recognized. Economic loss, family hostility and resistance, and legal concerns for inheritance are some of the barriers that prevent some couples from marrying. There is also the issue of who will have the final say when palliative care choices arise. But the same questions of identity, intimacy, and generativity that shaped the first two-thirds of life need to be answered: "Who am I? What will I do? With whom will I do it?"[13]

There's an absence of rituals concerning these issues for older adults and the "special" friendships in religious communities.

The present political struggle over "holy unions" as well as a movement for a constitutional definition of marriage has raised the risk level even for conversation about these matters. Many ordained clergy have been forbidden to use any authorized services as part of a ceremony for the blessing of (legally) non-sanctioned unions. Even to celebrate the news of these joined lives in a public worship service may be a chargeable offense in some traditions.

But why are clergy needed for a life-partnering ceremony? One person promises to love, care, and befriend another in the presence of their community. The classic pattern in Western Christianity for the proper *administration* of this ceremony had been that the couple married themselves.[14] The Celtic practice of "handfasting" is one example. The couple would pledge themselves to each other for a limited period of time, and both parties had the right to end the pledge at the end of this period. This practice was considered legal in Scotland until 1939 and has reemerged as the ceremonial pattern in non-traditional services. This contemporary pattern of clerical control of this ecclesiastical and civil hybrid ceremony has been described by James F. White as "a curious amalgam of Christian and pagan elements. . . . Weddings are a strange combination of Christ and culture."[15]

Should a community of faith be in the business of blessing partnership? The answer is yes when viewed from the intimate involvement that a community has in the lives of those who keep the promise to love and befriend each other. "Bear witness to the love of God in this world, so that those to whom love is a stranger will find in you generous friends."[16] Given this, there is both reason and need for a ceremony that will help to sustain this communal nurture and holy blessing for those who cannot be legally joined.

This ritual is based on the premise that it is possible for two people to give themselves into the care of each other, their loved ones, and God, without misusing the authorized liturgical rites of a tradition or requiring legal permission. At the heart of this service are two people, old enough to know what they're doing, who link their hands and lives together, and say "We will," in the presence of those who will bless, love, and support them.

Ritual for Life Partners

Greeting to the Beloved Community

The family and friends are welcomed by the couple into either one of their homes or in a room reserved in a restaurant where they often eat. In the center is a table with a bottle of wine, a dish of salt, and a small bowl of oil. The service is printed on a single sheet with a picture of the couple.

Couple: Your presence here is a blessing to us. We hope we have been and will continue to be a blessing to you.

Community: We are blessed and bless the One who created you and sustains you in health, joy, and peace.

Couple: (*facing each other*) Let us tell you what we mean to each other.

This can be spontaneous or they can take turns saying the following:

We are not our own. We belong to God, to our families, and this community.

We are not alone. We have chosen each other.

We want to make a place of welcome out of our lives.

I hope to offer you shelter as we risk the unknown.

I hope to offer you support as we remember our past.

You are part of life that's worth living. (*repeat*)

I want to pray for, learn from, and grow older and wiser with you. (*repeat*)

In your presence, in this community we want to make a promise.

They turn to each other and repeat one after the other:

Couple: I promise to do everything in my power to uphold your life.

Community: We promise to do everything in our power to sustain your love.

Readings or Music

Members of the community may share brief readings or music.

Gifts for Community

The gifts are presented by friends with the following words:

The gift of bread so that you will continue to practice hospitality.

The gift of salt so that you will continue to know the ways of peace.

The gift of wine so that this joining of lives will bring you great joy.

Anointing of Hands *(read by a member of the family)*

When hands are joined, promises are made and lives are changed. Offering your hand to another is an ancient gesture of friendship, love, and acceptance. Our hands are the means of our work and love. God's healing touch can be felt through the gift of your hands.

Oil is a sign of the Holy Spirit, used to heal, to bless, to seal the gifts of God. As you anoint the hands of your partner remember he/she is God's creation. Whatever good you would make of your love, make with your heart and your hands in honor of Christ, the Anointed One.

*The youngest person present offers the couple the bowl of oil
and holds it as they say:*

N: I anoint you with the oil of gladness and joy.

N: I anoint you with the oil of gladness and joy.

Together: For life . . . for life . . . hold on.

Prayer of the People

Men: Maker of the universe,
                designer of heaven and earth,
                You created us of dust and breath
                and placed in our hearts
                a longing for another, our partner,
                our lover, our friend.
                You taught us the mysteries
                of faith, hope, and love,
                and claimed us for a world that needs to see
                faith, hope, and love in action.

Women: Live in them.
                Grow them in wisdom.
                Show them grace.
                Be the heart of their hearts,
                and the life for their lives
                so that they may be for the world
                the beloved of God.

Blessing of the Couple

*The oldest person of the community holds the couple's hands
and says:*

                Celebrate this partnership.
                Allow it to grow old wisely.
                Hold on to its grace and possibilities
                and always commit each other into God's hand.

Community: May it be so.

A meal follows the service and the bread, the wine, and the salt are shared with the community. The oil is saved for anointing.

Adaptability

This ceremony was created almost twenty years ago for a particular couple. It is a ceremony that is designed to give leadership to a couple and their community. The text can be altered or dispensed with altogether. Holding and anointing hands, asking for a blessing, making promises, and sharing a meal with the community are at the heart of this ritual. The ceremony is not intended to create or establish a legally recognized change in the status of the couple. It could also be used for the renewal of vows for a previously married couple.

3

Partnering with Community
Giving Up the Car Keys

LINDA J. VOGEL

"Betty" spoke with deep feeling as she shared this story with participants at a workshop entitled "Growing Old: The Power of Story and Ritual."[17]

My two sisters and I had a call from a longtime neighbor who said, "I really think your mother shouldn't be driving anymore." This call confirmed what my sisters and I had been thinking but putting off. I knew it was time for drastic action.

Since our father's death, Mother had adjusted well and prided herself on going places and on being able to pick up friends who didn't drive. She treasured her independence. My sisters lived several hours away, and I lived across the city. We all went home as often as we could to help Mother do what needed doing to keep up the house and yard. After several long phone calls to each other, we had a plan.

Since I was the eldest daughter, it was my task to tell Mother we were all coming home the next weekend. Her first reaction was "That's wonderful!" And then she must have heard something in my voice because she said, "What's wrong? Why are you coming home?" I told her we needed to talk some things over with her but not to worry (vain hope!).

We all arrived early Saturday morning and invited Mother to join us at the kitchen table, where, over coffee, hundreds of family conversations had gone on before. I was elected to deliver what we knew would be devastating news. "Mother, we've known and you've known for some time that the day would come when it was time for you to give up your car keys and stop driving. That day is now." She looked at each of us in turn and saw resolute concurrence. "But I'm so careful," she said. "And I go slow and always look both ways — always."

One of my sisters said, "Mother, your reaction time is much slower than it used to be. And sometimes going slow is a hazard, too. We just want you to stop before you have an accident or hurt someone else. It really is best!" And then I said, "We're going to cook up a storm today because tomorrow the whole family and our next door neighbors are coming for dinner. Remember how many times we've all spent Saturdays each making our specialties? That dining room table will be groaning tomorrow!"

We cooked and shared memories and laughed and cried with our mom. She tried to be brave but we could see what a hard time she was having. And it seemed a little unfair that it was three to one! By suppertime, there were pies cooling on the back porch and the good china had been set out on the large oak table in the dining room. We all slept a little restlessly and were up early to get ready for dinner.

I went to church with Mother, and my sisters stayed home to get things ready. We had called out the troops, and soon our husbands and teenaged and young adult children began arriving. The families on both sides of Mother's house had lived there as long as we had, and several of our lifelong friends heeded the call to come as well. This meal would provide us a time for sharing stories and laughing and crying as we all grieved our mother's and grandmother's and next door neighbor's loss of independence.

After the pie had been served, I said, "This is a hard day for Grandma, but it is an important day too. We are here to remember with her all the ways she has helped us by taking us where we needed to go."

And then we went around the table, remembering together. Gladys said, "Edith, remember when Joe was out of town and Jenny fell and cut her leg and was bleeding so badly. I called and you said, 'Wrap it in old towels — I'll be right over. And you drove us to the emergency room.' Then Jenny piped up and said, "You were always our favorite carpooling mom because you never yelled at us when we ate in your car or even when we were late."

Martha, who lived on the other side of us and had been widowed years before, said, "You helped me so much by dropping in for coffee after George died, and you would take me to the store or out for lunch. You just seemed to sense when I was the most down. I don't know how I would have made it without you."

Grandchildren spoke up — recalling times when Grandma had picked them up and taken them to her house for special weekend visits. Once everyone had had an opportunity to share a story or a memory, I said, "Today is a hard day for all of us, because today we are asking Grandma to give up her car keys and not to drive her car anymore. It is both sad and scary. So I would like to invite each of us to offer her words of comfort and hope."

Gladys was the first to speak. "I always grocery shop on Fridays. I will take you with me, and then we can go out for lunch together." Grandson Tommy eagerly jumped in. "I just got my license, Grandma. Just call and I'll be glad to run errands for you or to take you wherever you want to go. I love to drive!" And so we went around the table. Some spoke words of thanksgiving for past experiences; many made promises to help Grandma be able to remain in her home and still go to the places she needed to go. One of my sisters said, "Since we live farther away, we want to give you coupons so you can use 'dial-a-ride' whenever you want to go shopping." My husband said, "Mother, you know I have quite a bit of flexibility in my work. Call me whenever you need to go to the doctor, and I'll pick you up and go with you."

Finally, the coffee pot was drained, the grandsons had finished their second pieces of pie, and the time had come for Mother to give us her keys. She wiped a tear from her cheek, and then she handed her keys to me. And then she said in her own gracious way, "I'd like to pray now. I want to thank God for family and friends who bring me so much joy and who will always be there when I need them."

Later, as Mother and we three sisters were finishing up the dishes, we began talking about who should bring what for this year's Thanksgiving dinner. Mother said, "Now don't any of you get it in your head to say it's too much for me to have Thanksgiving here! This is our home and I want to stay here and to have the family here for a long time yet!" And we said, "We'd like that, too, Mother. We'll do everything we can to help make it happen."

Ritual for Giving Up the Car Keys

Breaking bread together around the table is perhaps the most significant Christian experience that families and friends can share. Jesus shared many meals with friends and with those who may have been seen as enemies — those at the wedding at Cana, Mary and Martha, Zacchaeus, his disciples, and the five thousand who came to hear him preach and to see him heal. After the resurrection, he broke bread with the two disciples in Emmaus, and he shared breakfast on the shore with his disciples.

Edith's daughters sensed that when the family had to insist that she give up driving, gathering around the family table was the right setting in which to give thanks for the past, to act in the present, and to offer promises and hope for the future.

The ritual meal with story sharing, the ritual act of handing over the keys, and making promises can provide a model for others who find it necessary to name and act in response to a significant loss.

Preparing the Meal and the Table

Preparation that includes *remembering* and *sharing* in a familiar and comfortable setting can be an important part of the ritual process. Fixing special favorite recipes and using the best dishes and silver can all contribute to experiencing this as an important (sad or happy) celebration.

Gathering around the Table to Share a Meal

Those with whom this loss is to be acknowledged and shared gather at the table where grace is offered and the purpose for which the family has gathered is named. Bread is broken and stories are shared in conversation.

Inviting Family Members to Share Stories Related to the Loss Being Acknowledged

All who wish share stories or offer thanks for past experiences.

Confirming the Recognition of the Loss with a Symbolic Act

In this case, Edith gives her daughter her car keys.

Promising to Respond to the Loss in Creative and Helpful Ways

Those who can offer acts to help compensate for the loss do so.

Offering a Prayer Acknowledging Both Grief for the Loss and Hope for the Future

In this case, Edith wanted to offer this prayer. In other cases, it could be offered by one of the daughters or another appropriate person.

Gathering Up the Leftovers

We find a clue when Jesus instructed the disciples to "gather the leftovers" after the five thousand plus had been fed from the two fish and five barley loaves. Including Edith in this time with her daughters offered opportunities for more remembering. Edith expressed her fear that her daughters might take away her ability to hold family celebrations, and they were able to reassure her that, in the foreseeable future, they could help her maintain this important role.

Adaptability

This is one example of a family ritual around a significant loss sustained by the matriarch of the family. Each family can adapt such a model to address its own particular situation, family history, and needs.

Create a safe and comfortable environment if at all possible. The setting for this ritual was around the table in the woman's own home. Other places would also be appropriate: the living room or family room, another family member's home, an outdoor setting. At some time during the ritual, it is important to name the family's history with the vehicle and the woman's sense of independence and control over her life through access to the vehicle. Family and friends (as well as the woman) may need to express their fears over what might happen if the woman continues to drive the car — an accident that might bring harm to the woman or to others on the road. The keys are the primary symbol for this ritual, and giving over the keys, signing a document to transfer the title on the car to another person, or some other act functions as the symbolic action for this ritual. Prayers, words of commitment to drive her where she needs to go, even a song may be appropriate for the occasion.

4

"When We Must Bear Persistent Pain"

RUTH DUCK

The idea for "When We Must Bear Persistent Pain" came in Collegeville, Minnesota, at the 2004 Hymn Society meeting, while missing sessions because of migraine headaches — so far a disease that can be controlled but not cured for some of us.

When we must bear persistent pain
and suffer with no cure in sight,
come, Holy Presence, breathe your peace
with gifts of warmth and healing light.
Support us as we learn new ways
to care for bodies newly frail.

Help us endure, and live and love.
Hear our complaint when patience fails.
We thank you for the better days
when we may smile to greet the sun
to do our work with clearing mind
and bless your name when day is done.
In pain or ease, in life and death,
to you our fragile lives belong,
and so we trust you in all things.
You are our hope, our health, our song.

— Words: Ruth Duck, copyright 2004
Tune: JERUSALEM (Charles Hubert Parry, 1916)

Chapter Two

Being Changed

Aging is our primal experience of the word "Change." We spend most of our life trying to negotiate the intransitive senses of this word/experience. We discover, often without wanting to, what it means to:

- become different
- pass from one phase to another
- shift one's means of conveyance

- shift to a lower register
- undergo transformation, transition, or substitution

The chapter contains life stories and rituals that help to structure the changes that aging requires. None of these rituals is intended to be set in stone. They are all living documents of a particular context of particular women. They are sign/acts to show us the way as we struggle to live wisely and love well in the midst of body-shaking, soul-reshaping, and sometimes heart-breaking times.

5

Change of Life
A Flash of Insight

SUSAN K. ROLL

In the first panel of a popular comic strip, the central character, a middle-aged woman coping with hot flashes, exclaims to her friend, who had definitively proclaimed that she would never use hormone replacement therapy, "What happened? I thought you said you went herbal!" Her friend conceded, "Yes. Until I went crazy."

The "change of life," as our grandmothers called it, never enjoyed a great deal of public attention or support and, apart from occasional contributions to awareness such as the comic strip mentioned above, still does not. Women might informally share information, experiences, and remedies, trade self-help books, or talk over which doctor recommends which strategy (and then go off and try it). Yet women's personal experiences vary greatly: one woman's experience of serious damage to the quality of life or health might not resemble anything that happened to her mother, or indeed to her friends.

Menopause generally occurs between the ages of forty-five and fifty-five. Although menopause marks a definite passage in time characterized by an awareness of the first unmistakable signs of age, it need not stamp a woman as "old" — perhaps more "in the middle." The same period of life may be marked by a twenty-fifth wedding anniversary or a twenty-fifth high school or college reunion. If one has children, they may become visibly more independent; they might themselves marry and have the first grandchildren. At the very same time, one may be caring for aging parents, or facing the fact that the generation of one's parents and aunts and uncles is dying, so the "buffer" between one's own generation and old age is disappearing. Perhaps suppressed secrets from one's earlier life start to nibble at one's consciousness: sexual or other forms of abuse, lingering resentments, an emerging different sexual orientation, a secret adoption or abortion, or simply old arguments never resolved or relationships broken. One might worry about financial security with retirement on the horizon or the continuing financial burdens of the family. One's hopeful dreams and grand-scale plans may have faded or been forgotten.

Menopause means you finally have a womb with a view.
—Tamara Murray

Menopause, however, is an embodied passage: one's hormonal balance shifts and fertility abates. A woman might feel distress at the loss, joy at the freedom, or a bit of both: the body might mourn for children not borne or exult in its liberation from the possibility of pregnancy. Many women undergo months or years of hot flashes. Cheerful optimists might name them "power surges"; others call them just plain hell on wheels. One may experience memory lapses, lack of concentration (a logical outcome of loss of sleep due to hot flashes), difficulty in keeping weight off, thinning hair, dryness, fatigue, the beginnings of creaky joints, or perhaps more pronounced depression or anxiety. The body has a mind of its own, so to speak.

Yet at the same time, given a normal life span, there is plenty of time left to set a new course, develop new skills, pursue a dream, or find ways to release creative energy. One can begin to integrate knowledge into a deeper level of wisdom. Time in fact marks the spirit of this passage: time already traveled to gain experience and wisdom, time remaining to express wisdom and pass it along; time in a progressive trajectory, yet time that cycles around and comes to completion, while bearing the seeds of new beginnings.

A Rite of Passage for Menopause

In contrast to other plans for menopause liturgies that employ the colors red or purple to signify blood,[18] I planned this rite around coolness and calm. When my body suddenly went super-nova at regular intervals all day and all night, the last thing I could stand was any reminder of heat: I did not want to live in this burning body at the moment and didn't particularly want human touch either. When the *yang* of violent heat threatens to overwhelm you, the restorative *yin* of cool water, light colors, and gentle music and speech can bring balance and peace of mind.

Begin by setting up a meditative space with an abundant amount of flowing water in the middle. Outdoors, this could center around a fountain, or a (clean) fishpond or birdbath, and indoors, perhaps a battery-operated fountain to provide a refreshing splashing or burbling sound. You could also place on a round table a large glass bowl of water with flowers floating on the surface or a few floater candles. The water might be subtly scented with lily of the valley or another light floral or citrus scent. Seats for participants should be arranged in a circle around the water.

The time of the ritual is early evening, just past the heat of the day, in the shelter of twilight. As participants assemble, offer them a cool drink (herbal iced tea, flavored bottled water, club soda) and have them take a seat around the water. Invite all those present to share a thought or a reflection concerning menopause: it might be wisdom or advice from older

women, solidarity and understanding from women in menopause themselves, or anticipation and concerns from younger
women. When the conversation begins to die down, allow a
few moments of common meditative silence; then one person
addresses the group in these or similar words:

> [Name], today we gather to walk with you a new part of
> your journey. Your body is passing over into a new reality,
> a new form of incarnation. Body, mind, emotions, memory
> all together enter a fresh and unfamiliar territory and em-
> brace a different form of being. We cannot be part of your
> body, and we cannot take away the less pleasant parts of
> this new being. But we can wrap you in a cocoon of song,
> story, and blessing, to invite you to emerge transformed,
> healed, integrated, strengthened, and at peace.

Some form of participatory music follows: unison singing of a
simple refrain several times over, or with verses sung or spoken
by all or by one cantor, perhaps accompanied by a simple instrument or drums (which can be improvised from pots, barrels, or
anything at hand that resonates). Alternatively the group could
hum for several minutes: each person chooses a comfortable
tone and just hums the note, louder or softer, in the rhythm of
breathing, swelling and abating naturally.

*There is no more creative force in the world than the
menopausal woman with zest.*   —Margaret Mead

For the "word" component of the ritual, several approaches
are possible. Unfortunately the Hebrew Scriptures and the New
Testament provide only ambivalent stories of women in post-
menopausal infertility: Sarah and Elizabeth. In both cases their
"barrenness" was considered a curse and their late-life pregnan-
cies a triumph, a poor paradigm for entering into and accepting

the cessation of one's natural fertility cycle. The Psalms provide better material if a text from scripture is desired: Psalm 90 if the emphasis is on gaining wisdom with advancing age, Psalm 38 or Isaiah 38 if the woman in menopause has experienced a process of physical distress followed by relief or healing. A passage from the Song of Songs (on bodily delight) or an excerpt from chapters 6–9 of the Book of Wisdom might be used. A selection from the new hymn lyrics in Ward, Wild, and Morley, *Celebrating Women*, 117–35, could be read or sung, one of the Native stories in Daniels, *Changing Woman's Workbook*, could be recited, or any relevant story or poetry depicting change and transformation could be read.

As a follow-up, the woman being celebrated could share her own reflections at this point. Then all would keep a few moments of meditative silence together. The meditation could also be guided by gentle, unobtrusive recorded music, but this should be the only place in which recorded music is used, since its mechanical and distant nature detracts from the shared and intimate human spirit of the gathering.

The ritual or symbolic act of blessing this passage could take several forms:

- All participants gather in a circle around the water; each runs her hand through the water and gently raises it to bless the woman being celebrated, and each other, with a splash of water; or flowers floating on the surface could be tossed into the air, showering droplets of water.

- Each could take a handful of water to pour water into a jar or vase with flowers, or a large pot in which seeds are planted, or into a bamboo plant whose roots rest in small stones, as a sign of new life coming forth from water.

- Alternatively, a vial of a light-textured oil such as baby oil could be passed around by those gathered at the water to anoint the woman being celebrated and each other in blessing.

The rite proper would conclude with more music combined
with gesture or light-footed dancing in a circle around the
water, perhaps swirling diaphanous green, blue, or white shawls
or veils. The gathering of women might then share food and
continue their conversation and sharing: a light colorful salad
with an interesting texture of greens, fruits, and nuts, along
with whole wheat bread and tea. The group might also, with
tongue firmly in cheek, break and share with great solemnity a
bar of very good dark Belgian or Swiss chocolate.

6

Celebrating Change
Croning

BRIGITTE ENZNER-PROBST

"Croning" liturgies or rituals have received high visibility and provoked some theological controversy in recent years within the U.S. context. The term "crone" has many negative connotations. *The Random House College Dictionary* defines "crone" as "an ugly, withered old woman."[19] Merriam-Webster's definition leaves out the word "ugly" but the rest is given. It evokes images of lonely, old, even scary women. There are women in the third phase of their lives, however, who don't see themselves in this way and are reclaiming the word "crone" in its ancient usage as a "wise woman." Rather than seeing aging as something to be cursed, a necessary evil, these women celebrate aging, and the term "crone" is reclaimed, blessed, and celebrated.

A "croning ritual" honors those women among us who have reached a certain age (often age sixty). The actual year is not important. What is important is that the community gathers to honor a woman's age, to celebrate it as a milestone in her life; to respect the wisdom she has gained throughout her years — wisdom that she passes on to the next generations. During a croning ritual, her "cronies" gather (her friends and companions on the journey) and the woman whose age is being celebrated is blessed by being named "crone" — wise one.

Because the term "crone" has been associated with the ancient triple goddess image of "maiden, mother, and crone,"

Christian women who celebrate croning rituals are often accused of being "heathen" or even "witches." This has caused great controversy within the church in the United States. A croning ritual for Christians, however, simply celebrates an older woman's age by recognizing the wisdom that she has gained over the years and commissions her to share that wisdom with subsequent generations.

The croning ritual included below doesn't have the same baggage surrounding it as croning rituals in the United States because it was created in Germany in the context of a community of German women. It is *expected* that it will take place in a church building. And while the concept of celebrating aging was initially unfamiliar, the croning ritual was not associated in any way with witchcraft.

Croning Liturgy

When my friend, Ursula, always a busy woman, asked me to create a croning liturgy to celebrate her sixtieth birthday, I was taken aback by this idea. What? She wants to be called a "crone," an old woman, and we should celebrate the "oldness" of women, one of the worst things imaged by society? I had always known her as a lively and young, spirited woman. It was unthinkable for me to create a "croning liturgy" for her.

But after much conversation and sharing together, after reading some books on the topic and talking to several women who had celebrated such liturgies, I became acquainted with the idea of what it could be like to celebrate a croning liturgy for my friend.

First, we met several times. I listened as Ursula shared stories about her life and what was important, what was hard, and when she found joy. We spent a lot of time in conversation together since my friend had found the real thread of what this liturgy could be about — the meaning and importance of a rich and colored life. She wanted to name the "chasms" in her own life and the bridges that had been built to cross over these chasms. But she also wanted to recognize the chasms where women live in society, religion, family, and workplace and how we all can build bridges over these chasms. So this became the theme for the croning liturgy: Bridging the Chasms.

They [women] can aspire to be wise, not merely nice; to be competent, not merely helpful; to be strong, not merely graceful; to be ambitious for themselves, not merely for themselves in relation to men and children. They can let themselves age naturally and without embarrassment, actively protesting and disobeying the conventions that stem from this society's double standard about aging.... Women should allow their faces to show the lives they have lived. Women should tell the truth.[20]

— Susan Sontag

The next step was deciding how to develop this theme together with other women. We wanted to celebrate the croning liturgy in our parish hall. In anticipation of the event, we sent out invitations to many women. Later we prepared the parish hall with lovely cloths in various shades of blue. We placed a stool in the middle and covered it with blue cloths as well. We set up chairs in a circle around the room for the women who were coming to celebrate with us.

The croning celebration took place on a Sunday evening. After the women had gathered, we moved in a solemn procession into the parish hall, singing as we went. We led the crone to her blue throne. We all stood in a circle around her.

I opened the liturgy with a short prayer for the presence of the living spirit of God. Then we sat down and Ursula began to share stories of her life with all the chasms she had experienced and all the bridges she had built. With the naming of every chasm and bridge, she brought a symbol out of a basket at her side and laid the symbols down in a small circle around her. When she had finished sharing her story, she was encircled by the symbols of her life.

We clapped and started to dance around her, praising God for what had been given to her in her life and what had been given to us through her. After we were seated again, anyone who wanted could share the gift this woman had been in their own life. As these stories were shared, the women also offered symbols — small presents, flowers, stones, colorful cloths, bracelets — adding them to the circle of symbols representing her life. When everyone who wanted had shared, we once again danced around her in celebration of her life.

Then the woman being honored was given a pole. Connected to this pole were many ribbons of various colors. She lifted the pole high as each woman took the end of one of the ribbons and held it above her head. We were all connected to the woman in the center of the circle, creating a roof of ribbons over us all. Slowly we all began to dance. The "chasms" between us had been overcome. We felt a deep sense of connectedness and friendship. We danced and sang, forgetting time and space. Then we let go and the ribbons fell down around her like a colorful dress. I greeted her in her new status as crone — a wise mother for us all — and asked for her blessing. We hailed her and sang another song. After that Ursula offered a special blessing to every woman present.

Then, after a general blessing for us all, we began to go out from the hall in a merry procession. We danced and sang loudly. And long into the night, we ate and drank together.

Adaptability

Whose birthday is being celebrated? What is her age?

Who will be invited to the croning ceremony?

Where will the liturgy take place? In someone's home, in the church parlor or hall, outside?

When will the ceremony take place? On the birthday itself or a time close to it?

What will constitute the elements and organization of the ritual?

> *What* will the space look like? Colors? Fabrics? Chairs (circle, rows, square)? Flowers or other items?
>
> *What* symbols (if any) will be used? Symbols that represent wisdom? Symbols that represent the various aspects of the woman's life?
>
> *What* prayers will be offered?
>
> *What* songs (if any) will be sung?
>
> *What* poetry, readings, scripture, quotations (if any) will be read?
>
> *What* stories (if any) will be shared?
>
> *What* dancing will take place? By one woman? By the entire group?
>
> *What* symbolic action (if any) will take place? A blessing of the one being croned? A blessing for those gathered from the one being croned? The offering of gifts to the one being croned?

How will these various components be organized?

> *How* will the women gather? Will there be food available as they congregate? Will there be music playing in the background? Do the women dance into the space with the woman being croned leading the procession or does the woman being croned come in last?
>
> *How* will the croning liturgy begin? With a welcome? A prayer? Song? Reading?

How will the songs, readings, prayers, symbolic actions, and story sharing be organized? What will come first, second, third?

How will the formal part of the liturgy end? With a blessing? A dance? A song?

How will the occasion end?

7

Changing Roles
Becoming Orphaned

DEBORAH SOKOLOVE

It used to be unusual for people in their fifties and sixties to still have living parents. Today, at least in the industrialized world, it is increasingly common for people to live to see their great-grandchildren. For those who are pulled between the needs of ailing parents, children just beginning their adult lives, and their own aging bodies, it may be hard to imagine that one day they will be the oldest generation in their families.

For me, that day came early. My father died the year that I was twenty-two. His own parents had died many years earlier, and I have almost no memory of them. By the time I was thirty-four, my difficult grandfather and beloved grandmother on my mother's side had died as well. Two years later, my mother was gone too. She had cancer, which was both curse and blessing. The curse, of course, was the unrelenting pain with which she lived during the long months of her illness. The blessing was that, in her nights of wakefulness, she talked to me about her life with an honesty and intensity that had not previously been part of our relationship. It was as if the quiet dark of her living room — she wrapped in a blanket on the couch, me sitting in a chair close enough to hear her whisper — gave me permission to ask questions I had never before dared to ask, and her to tell the stories that, until then, had been locked within her heart.

Finally, after too many surgeries and too many rounds of chemotherapy, the doctors told me that the only thing they could do was to keep her comfortable. As she lay on the clean, white hospital sheets, she shivered with cold, and said she was afraid. I covered her with another blanket, held her hand, and assured her that she had nothing to fear, that I would sit with her until she fell asleep, and only then go home. A few hours later, I received a call letting me know that she had slept peacefully until she had breathed her last. I was thirty-six, a single mother with three children to raise. And now I was an orphan.

There was, of course, a funeral, at which aunts, uncles, cousins, and my mother's friends all offered condolences. My sister and I wept. We recited the prescribed prayers. I lit a candle in my mother's memory. And then everyone went on with their lives. I went back to work. I helped my children with their homework. But a gulf had opened between me and my friends, because there was no way to acknowledge that, in becoming an orphan, I had changed. I was alone, responsible, with no fallback position. I was the older generation.

Sometimes I feel like a motherless child. Sometimes I feel like a motherless child. Sometimes I feel like a motherless child . . . a long way from home, a long way from home.

—Harry Thacker Burleigh

It seemed to me at the time — and still does now, twenty years later — that a funeral is about the person who has died. It is intended, at least in part, to comfort those who mourn, but the focus — quite properly — is on the deceased. Although it is somewhat understood, it is never clearly noted that at least some of the mourners will now need to have a new self-understanding; they will be taking on a new identity. Spouses will be widowed; even adult children will be orphans.

During my mother's long illness, no one had prepared me for the fact that, after the initial shock of grief and loneliness, I would begin to feel a new weight of responsibility. I had become the head of the family in a way that simply hadn't been the case as long as even one of my own parents was alive. There was no ceremony, no ritual to mark this passage that our society tends to disregard. The loss of a loved one is noted, but not the gift of a new status in life, the need for a new way to understand one's role in the world.

At the time, I was not part of a community of faith. For the most part, my friends didn't know my mother and hadn't attended the funeral. Many of them had difficult relationships with their own parents and had no way to comprehend my sense of utter aloneness. What I longed for was a simple ritual — my friends gathered around me, listening to stories about my mother, telling stories of their own, and laying hands on me to bless me as I took on the unfamiliar role of elder in my family.

—DS

Adaptability

Deborah didn't have a ritual to help her deal with the reality of becoming the matriarch of the family. Since she was relatively young when it happened, she felt as if she had become orphaned. For older women, there is the knowledge, even expectation of some day (even soon) becoming the matriarch of the family. Regardless of one's age, however, there can be mixed emotions that accompany this transition in one's life. For some, they may have already assumed the role of matriarch of the family because the woman's mother is not capable of carrying on that role anymore. This transition takes place over time as the woman slowly takes over responsibilities that the mother usually had. In some families, the mother never really played this role; she was not dependable, not someone you could count on; she was not someone you felt comfortable coming home to when things went wrong in your life. But when a younger woman loses the last of her parents and feels "orphaned" and not ready to be the matriarch of the family, there are other emotions present. One has to grieve over the loss of a parent, recognize that there is no parent left to fall back on when things don't go well, and grow into a new responsibility within the family. When this is the case, a ritual can help the woman through this transition in her life.

The ritual should take place at an appropriate time after the activities of the funeral or memorial service have subsided. The woman's close friends and other family members (siblings, children, aunts, uncles, cousins) might gather in a safe, comfortable, and familiar environment.

Things to consider for the ritual:

- story sharing of the role the mother played as the matriarch of the family; the positive and negative aspects of being a matriarch within a family system

- grieving the loss of the mother and her generation

- naming how the woman depended on the mother in times of need and how not having that leaves a gulf in her life, a feeling of being orphaned

- naming her new responsibilities as the matriarch of the family

- expressing a commitment on the part of friends and other relatives to be there for her in times of need — to create a new "family" that will be there for each other

During this time, there can be readings (poetry, scripture, quotations), songs, and story sharing as seems appropriate.

8

Changing Self
Growing Stranger

HEATHER MURRAY ELKINS

. . . I was a stranger and you welcomed me.
—Matthew 25:35

When do we realize that we're aging? When we're confronted by a stranger who gets under our skin. We look in a mirror or a photo and see a face that's only vaguely familiar. *Red alert.* This response involves more than a refusal to recognize our own aging. It's a disassociation of body and self that is strengthened by a marketplace mentality, "image is everything." This fractured vision of women as "those to be seen" rather than as those who perceive cultivates an "I" dis-ease, an inability to conceive of oneself as *imago Dei* or as the beloved of God and the community. This is a visual infection, a distortion of identity triggered by unwilled transformation of the body/self from familiar to foreign. The first gray hair or glimpse of a sagging jaw line may trigger self-help rituals of resistance such as trying new cosmetics or surgery, refusing to be in family photos, or avoiding mirrors. This is so common a reaction that comics use it as standard material.

For women who are experiencing memory loss or any number of health problems, however, this "growing stranger" is a waking nightmare, not a comedy routine. We live in a culture where "personal value resides primarily in our capacity to think rationally and produce economically."[21] As long as we're able to explain ourselves and pay as we go, we can negotiate the fear of aging, make peace with the mirror or the family album.

It is the terror of becoming truly forgetful that makes us want to control this process of growing stranger. To be estranged from one's own history is seen as a sentence of solitary confinement. To be greeted by a stranger in the mirror can turn a familiar home into a prison. To be homebound can be a life sentence. It is here, therefore, that the emancipatory work of the gospel belongs: proclaiming release of captives and hospitality to the stranger.

The following rituals are designed to be used in ministry with those who are struggling with memory loss or dementia. The rituals incorporate images familiar to the one experiencing memory loss. At the core of these rituals is the biblical notion of redemption, which means "to purchase back that which has been sold into slavery" — the slavery here being memory loss or dementia. I also suggest using the term "memory-keeper" as an alternative to describing the woman only in terms of her medical condition.

Seeing Face to Face

Preparation

One of the first decisions is to determine what pattern of visitation would be most helpful for the woman in question. For some, visiting at the same time and day of the week will help set a pattern of expectation, but this expectation can turn to disappointment if the routine is not maintained. For others, a spontaneous visit works best. Consult with family or caregivers first. Friends or family members of the "memory-keeping" woman should first go through their own photographs that they have of her and bring them to share as part of this preparation. A small recorder, used unobtrusively but with permission, can record these conversations about her pictures. This is helpful

> *Even to your old age I am God, even when you turn gray*
> *I will carry you.*   —Isaiah 46:4 RSV

for reintroducing her to her own community. A selection of pictures from various times in her life could then be made. She may want to contribute to it from her own collection. These images can be scanned if she is comfortable in letting the pictures leave the house, or a scanner and laptop can be brought in as part of the regular visitation.

Sharing the images for several visits is suggested. The next stage of the ritual introduces the process of using the images to frame a mirror. A second set of the same images should be provided for the work. The mirror can be a new one or one presently being used in her home or room. Select images that are equally sized so that they will form a frame around the edge of the mirror. The pictures should be labeled on the bottom with names, dates, and places, if possible. Record each with a short history such as: "This is you in [year] at [place]."

Make invitations for a small gathering if that's appropriate for her. Make it clear that she doesn't need to feed anyone. Show her an invitation with the date and one of her scanned pictures on it that's been made and sent to her circle of friends and family.

Action

The guests each bring something to eat that she likes, and they announce their names as they arrive. The "face to face" mirror is placed in the center of the gathering. The photos are mounted on heavy card stock and Velcro so that they can be removed or changed as desired.

Passages from the Psalms and 1 Corinthians 13:12 can be read when the mirror is complete. If the memory-keeper likes music, make a CD with her favorite songs from different decades to be played as the pictures are shared. A tape or CD of her stories of her pictures can be played either now or in the future when she might not remember all the details of her pictures.

The mirror should be hung where she can see it every day. Form a circle around her facing the mirror. Close with this blessing or this rhyme spoken in union: "May Jesus, the fairest of all, give you the vision to see yourself as we see you: a beautiful woman of God."

or

Mirror, mirror on the wall,
Who's the fairest of us all?
[Name] is. Her name we call.
She's dearest and wisest of all.

A Family Table/Altar

Preparation

This ritual uses the same process of identifying family photos and preparing a mnemonic object or area that will serve to link ordinary images to personal identity with the help of a supportive community. The object in this ritual is a kitchen table. A conscious link should be made between this table and the communion table/altar of the community.

Action

Family photos are selected by the memory-keeper and copied, labeled, and arranged under a Plexiglas sheet cut to the size of the table. Words to the memory-keeper's favorite prayers or poems are arranged among the photos. These images and texts will help to anchor memories as she eats alone or guides the conversation for guests.

The ritual of the family table/altar could include a meal, one of the table graces, or a communion service.

Lost and Found

Preparation

This exercise is less a ritual than a ritualizing of the struggle of order over chaos. By inviting the community into a process of "everything in its place," some of the shame and panic can be removed from the process of memory loss through the work of play.

Action

Specifically designed craft boxes can be made during visits with the memory-keeper for the purpose of helping to regularize where commonplace things such as glasses, keys, and mail can be kept. Helping to make and cover these containers with fabric from the memory-keeper's collection will combine something new with something recognizable. Making marked containers for glasses, hearing aids, keys, and purse during regular visits helps to normalize conversation about memory loss while providing a way to resist it. Each box should be clearly labeled as to contents and placed in a convenient location.

Adaptability

Welcoming the stranger requires ceremonial patterns that will anchor memory and lower the fear factor of change. Studies on congregational religious attendance and participation demonstrate the need for a sufficient core of resources for public worship that prompt recognition of self and neighbor as well as God. Being able to recite the twenty-third psalm or the Lord's Prayer or sing one of the "good old hymns" by heart restores self in the midst of a changing community.

A faith community needs to extend its sacramental and ceremonial reach into private homes or communal living spaces. Seeing each other *face to face* can be a continual source of health and well-being. Outreach by the faith community into the sometimes estranged land of "homebound" or "shut-ins" is a primary form of hospitality for both parties: community and individual. The community's worship leaders could prepare for making these needed changes as part of a year-long theme on hospitality or entrust the changes needed to a women's group whose members include those who are experiencing this process of *growing stranger* and the need for this ministry of hospitality. There are essential actions/signs that can help those struggling with memory loss to feel welcome in a weekly service of worship. They can:

- Be encouraged to sit in the same place each week as an expression of witness, not a territorial claim. This can be stated during the time of sharing prior to prayer or as part of a sermon.

- Be offered a core of expected words, songs, and ceremonial actions of this particular community every week.

- Be given printed bulletins or service books or screen images that are legible for those with sight disabilities.

- Be greeted by those who repeat their names as they welcome them with their own.

- Be shown clearly marked facilities, for example, parking, restrooms, family life centers.

- Be offered assistance in transportation as a regular form of community outreach. One pastor routinely asks for those who need help getting home and those willing to give it before she delivers the benediction.

- Be reassured by the ritual closing of sign/acts such as "Now may the Lord bless you and keep you..." or a closing song that will signal the end of the gathering, as well as the promise that there will be another time to "see each other face to face."

9

"When Earth Is Changed"

RUTH DUCK

*...reflecting on the tragic death in a hiking accident
of Daniel Barnhart, the nineteen-year-old son of
my friend Norma Lee Barnhart*

When earth is changed and waters roar,
and mountains tremble, strong no more,
when tumult floods our lives, our homes,
God, be our help when trouble comes.

When death takes those we love the best
when illness robs our ease and rest,
O Holy Lover, hold us fast
as long as grief and trouble last.

When answers die on silent lips
and truth slips through our fingertips,
God, stay beside us in our hell,
that we may live the questions well.

God, keep us safe till peace returns
and raised from ashes, new hope burns.
Through change and tumult be our guide.
God, shelter us till storms subside.

—Words: Ruth Duck, copyright 1998.
Tune: L.M., DEO GRATIAS (United Methodist Hymnal, 267);
DUNEDIN (725); or GERMANY (415). Incorporating images
from Psalm 46 and Rainer Maria Rilke.

Chapter Three

Making Choices

Old age was once described by a world-famous leader, Golda Meir, like an experience of flying through a storm. "Once you're on board, there's nothing you can do." Yet the evidence of her life was to the contrary. She made choices that affected her community, her nation, and her world at every stage of her life. In this chapter we offer you a rich diversity of work from women who are artists and ritual-makers for themselves and their communities. Each piece is evidence of the power we have to choose life made in God's image and live it in the freedom of the glory of the children of God (Rom. 8:21).

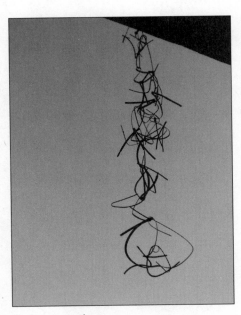

Underwire sculpture.

¿Hay una canción de la tercera edad?
Sí, hay una canción de la tercera edad,
y es tan hermosa y valiosa como la canción
de las otras edades que atravesamos por la vida.
A veces pensamos que nuestra canción ya no es válida
porque tal vez nos hemos jubilado de nuestra profesión
o porque tenemos canas.
Pero hay una canción única y especial en esta edad
que necesita ser cantada.
Esta es la edad cuando abundan los recuerdos y las experiencias.
Es la edad de la sabiduría de haber vivido.
Es la edad de reafirmar la presencia maravillosa
de un Dios que ha caminado con nosotras,
de un Dios que, porque hasta aquí nos ha bendecido,
nos da la certeza de que lo seguirá haciendo
los días y años por venir.[22]

— Clara Soto Ivey

Is there a song of the third stage of life?
Yes, there is a song of the third stage,
and it is as beautiful and valuable as the songs
of the other stages of life that we pass through.
Sometimes, we think that our song is no longer valid
because maybe we have retired from our profession
or because we have gray hairs.
But there is a unique and special song in this age
that needs to be sung.
This is the age when memories and experiences abound.
It is the age of wisdom from having lived.
It is the age of reaffirming the marvelous presence
of a God who has walked with us,
of a God who up until now has blessed us,
and so gives us the assurance that he/she will continue doing so
in the days and years to come.

10

The Woman Who Wouldn't Grow Old

A short story by
MARTHA HICKMAN

From the time she was five, Melinda Anderson determined never to grow old. Not old like ten, or even twenty, though when she saw in a magazine an ad for some cream for women who are approaching twenty-five, she shuddered. She might get to be twenty without looking old — but evidently at twenty-five, you needed potions.

She had nothing against old people. In fact they were some of the people she loved best in the world. Take her mother, for instance. Her mother had just had her fortieth birthday, and her friends had given her some crazy presents. One was a bottle of hair coloring. "Restore your Golden Locks!" the package read. Melinda's mother had dark brown hair, cut short and curled softly around her face. Melinda couldn't imagine her with golden hair. Her friend Marcie's mother had blond hair, but Melinda wouldn't want her for a mother. Another present was a big bottle of perfume that showed a picture of a man and woman lying close together on a sofa in front of a fireplace. Under the picture it said, "Keep those home fires burning." There was no fire in the fireplace — probably too hot, which was also why the man and woman weren't wearing much clothing. But Melinda thought if there was a fire anyplace else in their house they better get up off that sofa and go and put it out. Another present was a plastic cane, filled with small paper flowers. It had a big pink bow tied on the handle and as soon as the party guests went home, Melinda's mother let her try it out. Of course it came about up to her shoulder and she turned it upside down and pretended it was an umbrella handle and she was walking in the park in the rain.

By the time she was ten, she had moved her image of "old" up a few more years. Take her grandma, for instance. The whole family came together to celebrate her grandmother's return from a trip to China. Her grandmother was sixty-seven, and she wore a beautiful shiny black kimono with a pair of silver cranes embroidered on the back, and her dark hair was held back with fancy combs with sparkles at the edges. She didn't look old and shaky — not one bit.

That was the part that scared Melinda the most — looking old and shaky. She hadn't seen many people who looked old and shaky, but the one person she did see quite often was Mrs. Boyleston, across the street. She had gray hair, kind of frizzled around her face, and she sure could have used some of that cream Melinda had read about so long ago. Maybe she hadn't used it in time, because Mrs. Boyleston had celebrated her seventy-fifty birthday a few weeks before, and when you saw her up close, you could see more wrinkles than there are marks on a map.

At the party, Mrs. Boyleston had called to her, "Come on over, Melinda, and tell me what's happening in your life." She went over — she really did like Mrs. Boyleston — and when Mrs. Boyleston put her arm around Melinda's shoulder and pulled her toward her for a kiss, she felt her heart rise in gratitude. Mrs. Boyleston liked her, too. She kissed Mrs. Boyleston's cheek. It felt soft and warm, not dry and crackly at all.

What to tell Mrs. Boyleston? Melinda was in seventh grade now and, along with most of the girls in her class, was infatuated with John Morris, the handsome blond boy with his hair brushed back from his face who knew the answers to all the algebra questions.

"Have you started algebra yet?" Mrs. Boyleston's question startled her. "I always loved algebra," Mrs. Boyleston went on, a smile making extra wrinkles around her eyes. "In fact I taught algebra in high school for three years after I met Mr. Boyleston." Her eyes twinkled some more. "Then I stopped. You know in those days if you were married you couldn't be a teacher."

"Why ever not?" Melinda asked.

"Maybe they thought you'd take a job away from a man, who might need it to support his family. It seems a silly rule, doesn't it? Thank goodness they've done away with such foolishness. "But" — she put her head back against the green velvet chair — "if you get stuck anywhere with algebra, you come to me, okay? Is it a deal?"

"It's a deal," Melinda said in a weak voice. "Thank you." And she wandered off to the nearest cluster of her friends to tell them about her talk with Mrs. Boyleston.

Almost, she thought to herself, she wouldn't mind so much if she could get old like Mrs. Boyleston.

Youth is the gift of nature, but age is a work of art.
— Garson Kanin

But then one day she saw Mrs. Boyleston walking out to the car with a cane. A cane! That was a dead giveaway that you were old, unless you used it for scaring away squirrels from the bird-feeder or pretending it was an umbrella.

"Hi, Mrs. Boyleston," she called out. "A lotta squirrels around these days, aren't there?"

No answer. Then she remembered. Her mother had mentioned at supper last night that "Sarah" — that was Mrs. Boyleston's name — "said she's finally decided to get hearing aids, says she should have done it years ago."

"Good for her," Melinda's father said. "Most people wait too long. Makes it harder to adjust to them. When my hearing starts to go, I'm going to get after it right away."

"I will, too," her mother said, laughing, "though let's hope it's not for awhile."

Melinda, who could hear every whisper the girls in school passed along about John Morris, looked at them and thought, What would it be like not to hear what people said to you? She'd seen people in church with these tan plastic half-moons behind their ears. Not me, she thought. I'm never going to have a hearing aid.

After she reached her teens, she had a cadre of girlfriends with whom — in school and on the phone — she exchanged the innuendoes of daily life: Who was dating whom? Who had already been invited to the junior hop? Who had the latest crush on the class president? Who was going to make it to cheerleader? Life had so many consuming adventures to observe, evaluate, watch for clues, good and bad, that the present was all she could — or wanted to — concern herself with.

Then it was off to college, and during her junior year she met Zan, who had transferred in from Rice, and they fell in love. Right after graduation they married, and any anxieties of what it would mean to be thirty years older were completely lost in the consuming pleasures and concerns of marriage and having Len and Carol and watching them grow. She scarcely thought about what it would be like to be sixty or seventy or even older. And while it was sobering when she reached forty, she thought back with derision at a book she had seen on her parents' bookshelf, *Life Begins at Forty,* and thought, That author must live in another world.

Just the same she scrutinized her face with extra care in the bathroom mirror. She had long since forgotten the name of that magically restorative cream she'd read about more than thirty years ago. Yes, there were lines out from the corners of her eyes, but when she complained to Zan that she was getting crow's feet and lines from the corners of her mouth down to her chin, he just laughed and kissed the crow's feet and said, "You're beautiful. When you get quivering jowls then we'll start to worry about it. Besides, you have a seventeen-year-old son and a fifteen-year-old daughter. And me! You can't expect to look like you're twenty-one."

She didn't mention that she had combed the cosmetic shelves in Walgreen's and picked an "Age-Defying Cream," which she had been using faithfully for six months, or that when she'd had her last appointment at the beauty parlor she'd acceded to the beautician's suggestion that she have her hair highlighted: "It's not a dye, honey, it just covers up any gray, gives your hair a younger, more lustrous look."

"Whatever it takes," she said laughing. Maybe moving up in years wasn't as ominous as she had expected.

Then one day she got a letter from the AARP. "No!" She threw it into the wastebasket as though it would burn her fingers. When did they start soliciting your membership? When you were about to turn fifty. "Retired persons?" Zan was a few months younger than she but no way was he planning to retire from the bank. And she expected to keep her teaching assistant job at the elementary school at least until the kids finished high school. Len would graduate next year but Carol had three more years to go.

She stared at the crumpled paper, the distasteful evidence in the wastebasket. With a sigh she reached down and retrieved it. "I'm going to be fifty anyway — might as well avail myself of the privileges." She remembered her mother and father getting out their AARP cards when checking into motels. And the movie theaters always posted lower admission for seniors.

Of course she had lots of friends her age, and they talked about all the things they did to keep aging at bay — exercising, a whole round of diets, crossing the street to avoid going by the chocolate shop. They laughed as though it was almost a joke, not that serious — yet.

Then the talk would shift to their children — who was finishing college, or starting, or getting married, or divorced. There was a good deal of clucking about the music of the day and speculation about who was going to become a grandmother.

"Grandmother!" Something in Melinda's heart turned over at the sound of the word. Sometime, she supposed, she would become a grandmother. But not yet — though grandmothers seemed to be getting younger all the time. Carol, a sophomore at Smith, had a serious boyfriend and they had talked about getting married. Len seemed to have a different girlfriend every time they visited him at Williams.

It was all right until she got to fifty-six. Fifty-five had been bad enough, but once you entered the second half of a decade, you were on the slide toward the next decade and before you knew it the years ticked by and there you were — another decade, another zero. She would be sixty.

She had tried to prepare for what was coming. She had attended several midlife seminars — at church or at the local hospital or the Y. They dwelled on the problems that accompanied menopause — which she had sailed through without a hot flash or mysterious mood swing. But still, the numbers were scary, moving you inexorably toward shrinking abilities and small but bothersome physical limitations. That had happened, too. Her knees were growing increasingly stiff and walking, especially downstairs, became a bit of a balancing act, so she always headed for a rail if there was one, and if there wasn't, she stayed close to the wall, so if she felt a bit wobbly she could lay the palm of her hand against the wall to steady herself. Carol had bought her a cane, but she refused to use it. "Not yet," she said and she put it in the closet. "Canes are for old people."

She saw lots of old people on the streets of her town. Once she saw a lady with gray hair riding a motorcycle! She began to feel a little stodgy by comparison with people she saw who must be about her age. If they didn't know it yet, they'd find out aging was no picnic — a long slide downhill. Maybe a new highlighting of her hair would do her good. She called and made an appointment for the next Thursday.

One afternoon as she was drinking tea and feeling a bit sorry for herself — she wished Zan *would* retire but he seemed wedded to that job at the bank — the phone rang. It was Len's wife, Sally, calling from Durham, fifty miles away. Sally was pregnant, but wasn't due for almost a month. Melinda had not allowed herself to dwell on it. So many things could go wrong.

"Hi, Grandma," Sally said, making no effort to hide her excitement.

"Sally! The baby's here?"

"As of one hour ago. Alice Melinda Evans. Seven pounds, three ounces. Say hello to your grandma, Alice, honey."

Melinda heard a faint gurgling sound. Tears stung her eyes. Then Len's voice came on the phone.

"Hi, Mom. What do you think of that? That was your granddaughter."

"Oh, Len. I'm crying, sweetheart. Congratulations."

"Me, too." She heard the snuffle in his voice. "Nobody told me being a father would be this wonderful!"

"Nobody told me being a grandmother would be this wonderful, either. When do I get to see her?"

"Can you and Dad come down Friday? You think you can manage the stairs?" Sally and Len lived in a second-floor walkup in the historic district, beautifully preserved but with notoriously difficult stairs — uneven risers, hollowed dips in the stone.

Melinda heard in the background the cooing sounds of the baby. "Of course I can." She looked toward the closet door and laughed. "Of course I can. I'll bring my cane!"

/ /

To Dye or Not to Dye

HEATHER MURRAY ELKINS

Why dye? I'd initiated a series of interviews with nineteen women in two retirement communities after reading a brief history of the hair coloring industry in North America. What cars are for men, hair is for women was the basic gist of the writer's argument. One can find evidence of racial, age, and gender diversity on the beauty section shelves, but class is also a motivational factor in the choice of hair product.

The public perception of women and hair and aging assumes a ritual: a woman spots her first gray hair in her mirror and laments, a ritual response. The changing color of hair or the loss of hair marks the inevitability of aging. The season of *senescence,* full maturity, has arrived. I wanted to explore women's responses and acts of resistance to this sense of inevitability. What was their understanding of this seemingly natural ritual act of dyeing hair? Hair dye is a healthier choice than the radical option suggested by P. G. Wodehouse: "There's only one cure for gray hair. It was invented by a Frenchman. It is called the guillotine."

The character in Martha Hickman's short story, Melinda, elects to dye her hair when the season of *senescence* arrives. Hair dyeing has historically been an act of agency, a means of laying hands on one of the most public expressions of identity, one's hair/head. I wanted to interview women who were in my mother's generation to get a sense of what symbolic and cultural meanings they associated with covering their hair/head. Theirs is the last of the formal hat-wearing generation of white women. Had wearing hats been an act of agency before hair dye had gone mainstream? I wondered what changes, if any, had opened up for self-expression and social expression.

The hat question seemed to lead nowhere. The nineteen women I interviewed stated that they'd worn hats because they had to and seemed uniformly glad when their culture mavens decided to shelve them. Several could describe hats that they remembered, however, and where and when they'd worn them.

These answers raised more questions about my mother's life of hats. She's in her late eighties and wears hats. That's an understatement. She has over a hundred of them, all hand made for her by others. I bought her a storage shed for them when she ran out of closet space last year. She didn't wear hats, however, until she hit sixty, so perhaps her act of resistance was to put on what other women were taking off.

She developed a certain style for getting old, using these hats as comic relief. People stop to talk to her in airports and on street corners. Of course if you're wearing a wide-brim hat with seventeen teddy bears on it or a hat that has small plastic figures that represent your favorite Christmas carols and you'll sing them if the stranger who stopped you can guess what they are . . . but I'm getting off the point here.

Women and their hair: to dye or not to dye. I asked each woman about the methods she used, whether she did her hair herself or had it done, her favorite product and color range and whether she was concerned about what others thought of her right to dye. Those who never dyed their hair, seven of the nineteen, said "No" to the question, "Does having gray hair mean that you're old?"(It should be noted that I did not ask the age of these women during the interview process. I was interested in individual oral histories rather than comparative statistics. Some volunteered the information.)

To those who did or had dyed their hair I repeated my basic question about motivation: Why dye? Their answers revealed more about women's relational identity than I'd expected. It was for their husbands, their children, and, in one case, for her mother. The woman who dyed her hair because of her mother stopped after her mother died. She summarized the reasons behind the dyeing relationship: "She couldn't handle my growing old." The common sense behind their answers was that they believed that the visible signs of aging needed to be resisted for the sake of those who loved them.

If truth is beauty, how come no one has their hair done in the library?
                                                        — Lily Tomlin

---

Only two of the nineteen women I interviewed in the retirement community on the subject of hair color said that they dyed their hair because they did it for themselves. One of the two said: "I want to, period." The other said, "I don't look good in gray."

There is certainly a biblical tradition regarding women and hair and head covering (see 1 Cor. 11:4–15), but no one I interviewed connected any theological or scriptural reasoning to their hair care. They were religiously grounded but made no connections between a woman's hair and the problem of attracting astral beings or unsettling the Apostle Paul's order of worship.

Changing the color of their hair did offer them *agency* in their aging. That agency was important to them in terms of relationship and social presentation. It was also important that this act of agency appear *natural* to the general public. They were less concerned about only their hairdressers knowing for sure since most, not all, had their hair "done" in their community context. "Hairdresser" was the preferred title for the one who worked on their hair, although some also talked about "beauty shops." The term "hair salon" wasn't used, nor was "barbershop."

The basic assumption that hair dyeing is now a culturally approved ritual undertaken by women in response to aging was

sustained in these conversations. The assumption that such action should not be obvious to the public eye was also sustained,
however. The need to respond ritually to this life situation was
not established since it seemed to be a matter of an individual,
rather than a corporate process, aside from being integrated
into the normal patterns of hair care. Public exposure or a communal witness was seen as undesirable. Agency in this life stage
was to be private, not public.

Two life situations may call for the development of rituals
of women's head covering or hair dyeing: loss of hair through
illness, or a ritual of recognition where community is created
using women's hair or hats as the symbolic core of the ritual.
I strongly urge a study of the biblical text of 1 Corinthians 11
as part of this ritualizing process for Christian communities.
The embedded patriarchal connections in these texts between
the "naturalness" of male leadership and women's lower status
are deeply rooted here. This distortion of the gospel continues
to misshape the full revelation of the *imago Dei* of women in
the church and the world. It's enough to make you want to tear
somebody's hair out or decide to go public.

A Story about Dyeing

I have dyed my hair for the last decade as an act of public
exposure. I'm a redhead by choice, not nature. The point is not
consistency since my color palate goes from fire engine red to
eggplant. It's agency, pure and simple. It isn't an act of resistance
to *senescence,* either, although I'm considering purple as the
color of choice when I turn sixty.

My hair color is a theological act of resistance, a public declaration of feminist intent. It didn't start that way. I was in the
Midwest, preparing to give a series of sermons. I'd been invited
by the pastor, but that invitation had come before I'd ended up
on a "No Admittance" radical right hit list. They were having
problems with their Greek versions of scripture. God's Wisdom,

in Greek, the term "Sophia," had become a codeword for detecting heresy. By the time I arrived for my first sermon, there was a hard core boycott. I wouldn't be allowed to use the pulpit. Since they were good United Methodists, however, I was allowed to deliver my testimony from the center aisle.

It was stressful, to say the least, to have to defend my right to call myself a Christian. The feminist label wasn't up for a vote. I think if you call yourself a feminist in public these days you are one. I wasn't looking forward to another two days of delivering the good news alive. I wandered into a beauty salon, thinking that a haircut would create a sense of order. I sat down, asked for a trim, took off my glasses, and promptly fell asleep. When I roused, I had a sense something had changed. My head felt strangely light. I felt my head and got a dangerously warm fuzzy feeling. My glasses only confirmed the worst. Buzz cut or POW special would sum it up. "Why?!!" was the only word I could manage. "Well," she said, holding her shears against her hip like a weapon, "you didn't say anything, so I kept cutting."

Staring in the mirror produced a surprisingly biblical experience; I felt shame. The second feeling was empathy with my friends who had lost hair because of medical treatments. I couldn't shake the notion that I'd been punished. It also crossed my mind that my hairdresser was a member of the congregation. I had only one option since wigs were out as were hats. "Dye it red," I said, "the wildest, brightest red you've got. I'd rather make the congregation think I did this on purpose instead of having a really bad hair day."

It turned out red, really red. It was radical. I looked like the flaming heretic they thought I was. It so unnerved them, however, that they didn't object when I walked to the pulpit. I don't think they heard a word I said; they just stared at my hair.

Explaining this to my colleagues and family was going to be a different matter. I bought my first hat to help me make an entrance into the family circle. It didn't work. My husband stopped mid-sentence when the hat came off. He couldn't think of a rational thing to say, he told me later. My seventeen-year-old son walked into the breach with a careful question. "Mom, if you were going to change your sexual identity, you'd tell us first, wouldn't you?"

I finally wised up. This hair dyeing, hair-raising experience is **agency** in bold face. A woman's hair is a measure of her identity in this culture, and I'd just found the way to upset the status quo. This was about politics and age, and class, and sexuality. This was also about theology, pure and simple.

Ritual Possibilities

1. **A healing service for a woman who's losing her hair due to illness.** Matthew 10:30–31 could be used as part of a litany. A woman may be invited to share her hair with those who will keep her in prayer and fellowship. There is an old tradition of keeping a lock of hair of loved ones and even weaving it into a pin that is worn over the heart.

2. **An Easter sunrise breakfast and hat-making event.** Use the skills of the elderly women in the congregation to create "Easter Bonnets" out of paper plates and craft items. Everyone participates and wears the creation to the early service. The communal delight in the leadership of these women and the willingness to engage in imaginative play will make memories that are at the heart of the congregation's identity.

3. **A hair-raising ceremony for women who will be facing a period of stress and anxiety.** This naming of "terrors" can be done through telling stories, painting images, or watching a movie together. One source of assurance comes from sharing laughter at the source of the terror; another can come from the calming effect of having one's hair brushed as part of a time of meditation and blessing. Psalm 23 can also be used with shared anointing of hair and body.

12

More Blessed to Receive

KATHY BLACK

Kay was a woman who was constantly giving to others. She and her husband were missionaries in Peru and Chile. She was a teacher, a counselor, a librarian, a spiritual advisor, a community organizer, and a healer in many ways. She gave to her family, the church, the community, and especially anyone in need.

Even after retiring, she spent another twenty years giving of herself to others. She worked with her church's Refugee Resettlement Committee helping over eighteen families become self-sufficient in U.S. society. Her church owned a house for this very purpose, and she dedicated many hours in making sure the house was always occupied. She helped numerous families navigate the legal system, find employment, enroll in school, learn English, and become adjusted to American culture. She was their teacher, guide, interpreter, and friend.

She was also very active in the women's organization, serving as secretary, mission coordinator, vice president, and president. She sewed dolls, was costumer for the local play, organized archives for the retirement home, was the driving force behind the Toy Committee, worked with Habitat for Humanity, volunteered at the Health Services Center in her retirement complex, and participated as an active member of two Bible study classes and a prayer group. She was dearly loved by many people.

At the age of eighty-four, she was diagnosed with cancer. She had melanoma, malignant lesions in the brain, and it had spread to her lungs and her liver. She was given three to six months to live. She could have kept it quiet, not wanting people to fuss over her, wanting to be stoic and independent until the end. She could have withdrawn from her community, living out her last days in isolation except for immediate family. She could have devalued herself because she was no longer able to give in the same way as before. But instead, she chose to share her condition with her friends, her retirement community, and her church family. And in doing so, she became as gracious in receiving as she was in giving.

The best classroom in the world is at the feet of an elderly person.
                                          —Andy Rooney

The Refugee Resettlement Committee in the church wanted to honor her life before she died so they planned a potluck dinner. They then decided to invite the women's organization as well and eventually opened the dinner party up to the entire church. Again, Kay could have resisted this dinner party, preferring to be "humble," not wanting people making a fuss over her, feeling somewhat embarrassed by all the attention, but she didn't. She graciously welcomed the community's overtures to honor her life, recognizing their need to ritualize her presence in their life and recognizing her own need to say good-bye.

The associate pastor and a few laywomen organized the event on the night of the regular Refugee Resettlement Committee meeting. Over a hundred people attended. The room was overflowing. There were decorations on the table, cards for people to write notes to Kay, music, and a time for various people to speak. Seven families who had been refugees and were resettled through the church came back to pay tribute to Kay. Students whom she had taught in Peru but who now lived in the area came to testify to Kay's influence on their lives. A neighbor at the retirement home spoke. One woman shared that she had been touched as a child when Kay and her husband came to talk at her church in Tucson when they were home from the missionary field on furlough. Former refugee families gave thanks for the tremendous influence Kay had on their lives. People spoke from the women's group, Habitat for Humanity, and the Refugee Resettlement Committee. Everyone was invited to offer Kay words of thanks and appreciation, words of celebration, memories of joy and struggle. Mindful of Kay's energy capacity, people were encouraged to keep their speeches short and to write additional reflections to Kay on the cards. At the end, Kay was offered a chance to speak and her words became the benediction. She thanked God for the opportunity to be a part of the church and to be of service to the world. She claimed the great circle of love that binds us all together in friendship and concern for one another and for all people. She expressed her love for everyone present and her gratitude for this occasion and basically said good-bye.

The people were extremely grateful for this opportunity to grieve with Kay and yet celebrate her life while she was still with them. Being able to say thanks helped the grieving process when she died two and a half weeks later. What many appreciated most was Kay's ability to receive as graciously as she gave. She actively participated in maintaining community to the very end. She taught many how to die with dignity and grace. The church community was able to surround Kay with love and gratitude before she died, to celebrate her life in Christ and for Christ, and to dismiss her with blessing in her next journey with God.

Ritual for Saying Good-Bye

Welcome and Purpose for Gathering *(by the associate pastor)*

Prayer *(of thanksgiving for Kay's life and gifts and service to the world and the church by the senior pastor)*

Breaking of Bread Together in the Potluck Dinner

Introduction of the Former Refugee Families

"Cuando El Pobre"/"When a Poor One" *(sung in Spanish)*

Solo: "If We Only Have Love"[23]

Testimonies *(a time for people to say thanks, to share memories, to celebrate Kay's life)*

Kay's Words of Wisdom for the Community

Adaptability

The book and movie *Tuesdays with Morrie* popularized this idea of having a celebration of one's life before one dies rather than waiting until the funeral. This type of ritualized celebration can take place with a large group in a church hall (as in the ritual above), or it can take place in someone's home with a few close friends and family members.

Key Ingredients

- a gracious and willing person who knows death is imminent
- people who want to give testimony to the person's life
- a recognition of grief and loss
- a celebration of the honored one's life
- a trust in God and God's presence in the journey now and beyond death

Optional Ingredients

- prayers: for the woman who is facing death, for the community that is grieving, for the world still in need of hope
- readings: favorite scripture passages, poetry, quotations, responsive readings
- songs: solo or corporate singing; favorite hymns or a song someone wants to offer in thanksgiving to the one being honored
- visuals: a visual portrayal of the woman's life, either photograph albums passed around, or slides or a video of the various phases and aspects of her life

13

Radical Choice
Losing a Part of One's Body

JANET WALTON

The New York Women's Liturgy Group gathered initially because the churches where many of us were members refused to take our experiences as women seriously. Even the smallest requests, such as eliminating the dominance of male-centered language as an experiment for a short time, were refused. Rather than leave our liturgical experiences angry and dissatisfied, we decided to do something constructive. Our earliest work addressed images and words about our relationships between God and community, a search for something new out of long-practiced traditions that were part of the very fiber of our beings. We focused on eliminating anything patriarchal, substituting instead stories, images, sounds, and actions that affirmed women's experiences. As we continued, month after month, we remembered not only our achievements but also our struggles. The liturgy that follows, which took place after I returned from having a bilateral mastectomy as a response to a diagnosis of breast cancer, is one example of the power of women's liturgies to provide support and hope in difficult situations and also to illustrate the relationship between faith and responsibility.

A mastectomy was not an easy decision, not before the surgery and not after it. It radically changed the appearance of my body; the scars remind me every day about a brush with death. I wanted to reclaim a new shape of my body in a world

> *Good liturgy always borders on the vulgar. The word "vulgar" carries here the connotation of earthy, as opposed to "refined." Good liturgy, if vulgar, is full of ambiguities, risk, "numinosity," sensuality, discomfort, and excitement. It contains the totality of human experience and places it, open to the future, before God.*[24]
>
> —Urban T. Holmes

that prizes a perfect female body. The liturgy focused on solidarity, an expression of love for me from those who gathered that extended to women far away as well (the *rebozo*, or shawl, was made by women in Guatemala). Central also to this liturgy was a commitment on the part of each of us to take our lives seriously in a world where women are at best undervalued and at worst objectified. We are responsible for our own choices, and those choices often come with a cost, even the loss of a part of a body. By inviting each other to remember when a choice cost something, we were empowering each other to continue to take a stand in relation to our own freedom and anyone else's as well. While the shape of a women's liturgy may be initiated from a particular need, it does not stop there but extends to everyone gathered. No one left this liturgy without thinking of the power she had to carry its power into the choices of daily living.

Liturgy after a Mastectomy[25]

One of the members begins the ritual.

Member: We're here because our friend has just had a mastectomy. We want to support her and help speed her recovery. We want to bless her so that her healing will be complete and as easy as possible.

Then follows a reading from Adrienne Rich (On Lies, Secrets, and Silence: Selected Prose 1966–1978 [*New York: W. W. Norton, 1979, p. 245]) that reminds us that we do not need experts to tell us about our lives. We know what is true and what is urgent. We can name our pain, our hope, and our questions. What we need are opportunities to remember, claim, and affirm what we know. What we need is to listen to ourselves and to trust what we hear. A member instructs the group.*

Member: Let's consider for a few minutes that deeply innate, merely physical life that surges through us in our bloodstream. It is hidden, unseen, needs no tending to on our part by voluntary attention, and it is the very course and stuff of life.

            Take a minute now to find your own pulse. Now help your neighbor to the left to touch yours, and let us sit for a moment in a circle of life, in touch with another's pulse, joined, silent, throbbing.

Now that all have felt the networking of our life, one of the group puts a rebozo, a large, soft, purple shawl made by women in Guatemala, a "mantle of caring," around me. A member offers me a personal word.

Member: In addition to the wish we have to unite our life with yours, we want to say in what admiration we hold you. You are a model of what it means to assume responsibility for tough decisions. We admire the way you let us into your crisis. You didn't shut us out as though it were not important to us or as though we needed to be spared. We admire the way you understood — or tried to understand — what your own needs would be: your need not to be fussed over, your need for privacy, your understanding that you might require help and that you would ask for it. And we want to testify that by your careful attention and pain in making a decision in the face of the few options open to you, you helped us all learn more about responsibility, maturing, and suffering, about our relationship to our bodies and what we can be to one another. So we salute you tonight.

Another reading from Adrienne Rich (On Lies, Secrets, and Silence, *p. 233*) *expresses well what the group wants to say to Janet. In it the members of the Women's Liturgy Group remind Janet (and themselves) to refuse to be silent while others speak in our name. Responsibility to ourselves requires us to claim our minds, to respect our bodies as inestimable treasures of particular and distinctive knowing. Responsibility to ourselves compels us to reject relationship in which we are treated as objects. Another member speaks.*

Member: But taking responsibility for oneself is not without cost. We can't even name the cost for another (sometimes we cannot even do it for ourselves); we can't name it for Janet. It's part of her hidden life, and we are not asking her to recount it.

But we will try to name some costs we ourselves have paid or how we understand being responsible for ourselves and the price it demands.

All share some silent time for reflection.

Then there is a "swapping of costs": each person describes a moment in her own life when taking responsibility cost something, for example, when speaking rather than being silent changed a relationship or challenged a job, when recognition of a destructive behavior required leaving what was comfortable. To conclude, each member of the community is invited to bless Janet: to touch a part of her body and bless it with her own words and gesture.[26]

All sing the "Song of the Soul" by Chris Williamson, a familiar song that expresses hope and healing, to conclude the liturgy.

Adaptability

The purpose of this liturgy is to name the loss of a particular part of the body, grieve this loss, and yet claim those other parts of the body that will still allow one to function in the world in whatever capacity is possible. In this liturgy, the woman chose to have both her breasts removed because of breast cancer. In another context, however, it may be the loss of a toe or foot or even leg through amputation from advanced diabetes, or the loss of one's ears if one becomes deaf, or the loss of one's eyes if one becomes blind. If one is using a wheelchair on a permanent basis, it may feel as if one has lost one's legs because they don't function in the same way anymore even though the legs are still physically present. (The ritual "Growing Stranger" deals with those who feel as if they are losing their minds, and we encourage you to consult that ritual's "Adaptability" section on page 81 if you would like guidance for a woman in this situation.)

To create a ritual for someone who has lost a part of her body, decide first what this person (or what her community) needs. Does she need to name the loss and grieve sufficiently so that she can accept the loss and take control of the rest of her body and her life? Or has she already dealt with the grief but needs to feel the support of the community around her, to hear them proclaim that she is still the person they know and love and won't avoid her or treat her any differently, that they will continue to be present for her in whatever ways are most helpful? Or is it the case that the loss does require a learning curve on the part of her community, that they need to treat her differently and they need to learn how to do it appropriately? If a woman can't hear anymore, her friends and family need to learn how *not* to talk to her like they always used to, to learn ways to communicate best with her. The ritual may be to provide an opportunity for her family and friends to commit themselves to these learnings and to be intentional about keeping her involved in the conversation. The same would be the case for someone who has become blind. For someone who has lost a leg, it may be necessary for family and friends to commit to transporting her to the grocery store, doctor's office, and church.

The ritual should be designed for the specific woman and her context. Once the focus has been established, the designers can begin to think about readings, poetry, scripture, songs, music, some sort of participation by the family and friends present (words of grief, words of affirmation of the other parts of the body that still function, words of commitment), or some kind of symbolic action that connects to her as well as each person present.

One woman, Marjorie Suchocki, chose to burn her bras as a symbolic act in response to her breast cancer. She was seventy-one when she had a bilateral mastectomy on April 1 — April Fool's Day. Marjorie chose "flatness" as her new look. Since she wouldn't need her bras anymore, she decided to have a bra burning party to thank all those who had supported her on her journey, to celebrate being cancer free, and to claim being "fashionably flat." Marjorie chose humor as her way of marking this crisis in her life. The invitations were sent to a Monstrous Regiment of Women with the instructions to BYOB — Bring Your Own Bra. She documented her journey by writing lyrics to a Christmas carol tune. Thirty-five women arrived with bras in hand. Other bras arrived in the mail from those who couldn't be present. A fire was built in the backyard, and the liturgy commenced. Candles were lit as names were called out: those who had died of cancer, those who were survivors, the 240,000 who would be diagnosed this year, and those who were the care givers. Marjorie's song was sung, poems written by guests were offered, the history of the bra was recited, and bras were thrown into the fire as the women chanted: "Ashes to Ashes, Dust to Dust, No More Underwire, No More Bust!"

The song Marjorie wrote is to be sung to the tune "Angels We Have Heard on High."

Chorus   Ouch and oh my gosh and ouch and oh my gosh and ouch and oh my gosh they're going. Bye, bye beauteous boobies.

Ouch and oh my gosh and ouch and oh my gosh and ouch and oh my gosh they're going. Bye, bye beauteous boobies.

Verse 1:   Once the skies were bright and clear,
Days were fine and easy.

Then a small cloud did appear,
turning tummy queasy.

Chorus

Verse 2:   First the needle pricks the skin,
this is called biopsy.

Doctor shoves that needle in,
pray he don't get dropsy.

Chorus

Verse 3:   Next a monstrous big cold knife
(this is called excision).

Marjorie, hold on to your life!
Surgeon, use precision!

Chorus

Verse 4:   Path report is not so good,
Marjorie starts a-sobbing.

Things ain't looking like they should,
boobs they will be robbing.

Chorus

Verse 5:   April Fool's Day rolls around,
Doctors, do your duties.

Soon I will be firmly bound,
bye, bye to my beauties.

Chorus

Verse 6:   Now you see I'm fashionably flat,
and I'm hale and hearty.

Let that be the end of that,
onward with the party.

Chorus

After the party was over, the ashes were cleaned out from the fireplace and a hanging sculpture was crafted from the burned underwires — a constant reminder of the fragility of life and yet the steadfastness of faith and friends. Each of these rituals can be adapted in a wide variety of ways.

The Willing of Things

KATHY BLACK with JEANNE AUDREY POWERS

Rev. Jeanne Audrey Powers is in her early seventies and the last person surviving on both her mother's and father's side of the family. The family line that she knew ends with her. She has no children and no living relatives to take responsibility of her estate when she dies. She has decided to make decisions before she dies and is in the process of determining the "willing of her things." There are seven areas of her life that need attention as she decides to whom she will give the financial and material elements of her estate. This process has involved a faith journey, a careful reflection on important relationships, a decision regarding "remembrance," the stewardship of resources, a legacy of hospitality, and an undergirding of causes for justice in the world—all of which will be active well into the future.

The Willing of Papers

Jeanne Audrey's life and calling began as a campus minister in Minnesota and continued for twenty-nine years in the United Methodist Church's national mission-sending agency and in ecumenical and interfaith offices in New York City. She was often in the midst of controversy — whether in her church's early feminist movement, in the National Council of Churches and World Council of Churches Faith and Order Commissions and their Ecumenical Decade for Women programs, in Palestinian interpretation and advocacy, in a new doctrinal statement on baptism for her church, and following her "coming out" as a lesbian. After appearing on national talk shows discussing inclusive language in scripture and rituals for people going through a divorce, she received over five thousand mailed responses from all over the country.

<hr>

So teach us to count our days
that we may gain a wise heart.
—Psalm 90:12 KJV

<hr>

Upon retirement, Jeanne Audrey "willed" these official office papers, documents, and files to the United Methodist Archives and History collection housed at Drew University. But numerous other documents, notes, and letters dealt with many personal issues about which she was deeply passionate, disclosing her own personal feelings about these issues. They had imbedded in them Jeanne Audrey's personality, perspectives, and vocation. Determining to whom these documents would be willed was a more difficult decision. Duke University's library courted her persuasively and now thirty-five feet of file boxes, plus her private papers beginning with her childhood, have become a part of their special collection dealing with women's history.

The Willing of "Chattel"

As is the case with many of us, most of the items in Jeanne Audrey's home have a story behind them or a memory associated with them. She purchased a variety of art pieces in her travels for the connections they have with people or countries or causes for justice. Some are family antiques that she grew up with and then inherited. Others were gifts from people on special occasions. She cherishes them: paintings, pottery, fabric, sculptures, carvings, jewelry, knickknacks, furniture, a doll, netsuke (tiny Japanese sculptures), and glass and handkerchief collections. She doesn't want them to end up in a yard sale or estate sale after her death.

So she is beginning to determine to whom she will "will" each item of importance. She likes to call all her possessions "chattel" — a legal term referring to an article of movable personal property. This is not simply because she wants her treasures to remain in familiar hands; it is also because she would like to be remembered in this way. In her own experience, when she has received a gift on the death of a loved one, the memory of that person has lived on every time she looks at the cherished keepsake. She receives much pleasure in knowing that her gifts will continue to be appreciated by her friends over the years as they remember her.

The Willing of Property

Jeanne Audrey has a double condo across the street from Hennepin Avenue United Methodist Church in Minneapolis that has been an integral part of her faith community and spiritual formation. She has willed the house to the church so that it can continue to be used for hospitality. A deep joy in her life has been offering her home to friends and strangers alike who need a place to stay. She would like this space to continue in ways it has already been used: to provide hospitality for an out-of-state family of a child needing medical care at one of the preeminent hospitals in the area, for people attending a conference in the city, for a woman in the middle of a divorce who needs to move out of her home for awhile, for visiting clergy from other countries, for traveling choir members or missionaries on furlough. She provided a list of over twenty different ways the condo has already been used in order to trigger the imagination of financially minded trustees.

In an attempt to broaden the church's understanding of its potential for ministry, the bequest is on condition that the property cannot be sold or used as a parsonage for a set number of years in hopes that the church will grow into their new opportunity for service.

The Willing of Finances

Determining how much money we will need to live for the rest of our lives, with inflation and deteriorating health, is so totally unpredictable that it is hard to decide how much to give away before we die and how much will be left to be willed to individuals or groups after we die. Several years ago, Jeanne Audrey decided to distribute some of her finances (previously included in her will) before her death. She wanted her inner circle of friends — her chosen "family" — to be able to enjoy it while they were younger and before her death. In addition to these individuals, she also donated a substantial amount to two theological schools (Claremont School of Theology and Pacific School of Religion) for specific social justice causes and scholarships. In each gift, with help from the seminaries, she created a new idea for implementation.

That taken care of, she still needs to make the final decision as to which groups, organizations, and institutions she will leave the rest of her finances. She wants her money to be able to make a difference to groups and organizations that are working for issues of justice in the church and society. The "willing" of her finances is an opportunity to participate in ministry and mission in areas she feels deeply passionate about long after her death.

The Willing of Her Body

Jeanne Audrey has decided that her body is one more item that can be willed. She has filled out the necessary paperwork at two medical schools so that whether she dies at her home in Minneapolis or her home at the retirement community of Pilgrim Place in California, one of the medical schools will be able to use her body for teaching or research purposes.

The Willing of Her Life Story

A while ago, Jeanne Audrey gathered some of her closest friends and asked them to participate with her in an exercise, a ritual of remembering. She knew that the time would come soon when she would write her obituary — what she wanted printed about her life after she died. It would be a short but final "willing" of her life's story. Around food and conversation, she asked her friends what they thought should be included in her obituary. A person was designated to take notes so that the comments and stories would be accessible when the time came to do the actual writing. As each shared what they thought were crucial elements and contributions of Jeanne Audrey's life, storytelling was shared and the remembering was imbued with laughter and pride.

When we die we leave behind us all that we have and take with us all that we are. — Anonymous

In addition to her obituary, Jeanne Audrey is also designing her memorial service. While the obituary will name her life's story and *what* she wants to be remembered by, the memorial service will set the tone for *how* she wants to be remembered. Her theological perspective on death and resurrection in the service — the tone of the music, the scriptures, and the poetry, the testimony of the preacher, and the stories shared by people chosen to witness to her life — will all proclaim to the world how she lived, what she believed, and how she wants to be remembered.

The Willing of the Tombstone

Since the late 1800s Jeanne Audrey's mother's family has had a family cemetery plot in Mankato, Minnesota, that was an important part of her childhood. She would visit the cemetery nearly weekly with her grandmother, aunts, and parents. While the adults weeded around the graves, Jeanne Audrey would "play" by wandering around and reading the tombstones. She was touched by the multiple deaths of children in the same family, the names of people that matched early street names in the town, the dates and sayings that conveyed something about the persons buried there. Since Jeanne Audrey is the last of her family, she intends for what ashes are left of her body (after the medical school has completed its work) to be spread over the family plot. But she would like to "will" to the community one last tombstone that will name the end of the family tree and yet say something personal as well:

> *The last of the Jones family*
> *Niece of Grace and Edna*
> *Granddaughter of Lizzie*
> *Daughter of Florence Jones Powers*
> *JEANNE AUDREY POWERS*
> *1932 –*
> *Subversive to the End*
> *Visionary and Prophetic*

Adaptability

A ritual can be designed around any one of these occasions for the "willing of things." A celebration of memories can be designed as a woman gathers the future recipients of her "chattel," tells the story of each item, and tells each person why she wants her or him to have the item after her death. The items themselves can be the symbols of the memories.

A woman can gather her family around her as she explains how she wants to donate her body to a local medical school for research and teaching purposes and then sign the appropriate documents as a symbol of her commitment. This can be done with her finances as well, if gifts are to be given to institutions or organizations.

She can invite family members, a few close friends, and her pastor to gather as she shares her desires for her funeral or memorial service, and together they can work on the design and the content: prayers, songs, poetry, liturgical dance, music styles, scripture passages, testimony by a select few or by any present. She can also let it be known who she wants to participate in the service.

Creating Community
Rituals of Recognition

HEATHER MURRAY ELKINS

Many contemporary women cannot assume that they will live the last season of life in the physical presence of either family or a traditional community that has known them over time. Many women will spend the last years of their lives in communities that they have chosen or that have been chosen for them, such as retirement communities or extended care facilities. Rituals that will provide "credibility, guiding metaphor, and emotional resonance for those involved," are essential to the quality of life of women who can reasonably expect to live together in community.[27] These rituals of recognition assist in the creation of new communities of nurture and support for women who join them in the last season of life. Faith communities and women's groups should consider using these as part of their regular gathering in order to enhance their knowledge of each other and in preparation for the time that they might need to be recalled to themselves by the ritualized use of music, recitation, or actions.

When we were young, learning to dress ourselves was one of the primary lessons in growing up. Learning to tie our shoes, figuring out how a button worked, learning the mysteries of a zipper became essential gestures for human community. We were taught these things at home, in school, by our parents and older siblings. Clothing is an ancient and contemporary expression of human culture; we find evidence in rock paintings, tombs, hope chests, fashion magazines, and even the book of Genesis. The ability to dress oneself is seen as a necessary measure of social control and mental ability. The very young strive to master it and the aging struggle against the loss of this hard-learned ability, partly because of the human dignity that depends on being able to "dress."

Once upon a time our fingers were unskilled with buttons because we were young. As we age, we often find the task difficult again because of stiffening fingers or loss of sight or not having anyone to sew them on again. These everyday buttons, therefore, begin to take on a greater significance than simple ornamentation. They have biographies, concrete histories of private and public life. They are the holy human stuff that holds our memories, our ability to make meaning, and our clothing together.

The following ritual is designed to evoke the wealth of memories that are "buttoned down tight" in our sense of self and others. It combines brief narratives of the history and meaning of buttons in Western culture with a chant and a game that many may remember from their childhood. The intention of the ritual is to elicit memories and create community for women who may or may not know each other well. It can be offered as part of a study on biblical topics, as a spiritual exercise in a retreat setting or in a secular women's group, or as a ritual for women who now share the same living space with other women because they cannot or choose not to live alone.

Button, Button, Who's Got the Button?

Gathering

Large bowls of buttons as well as strands of yarn, each threaded with a big needle, are placed on a table at the front of the room. Images of women's fashion from a diversity of times and places are on the walls. Music welcomes those who arrive.

There should be space for seating small circles of four or five people each with space for the readers to be at the front or in the center of the room. The Button Liturgy is on the chairs in each group. Someone should begin the introductions of names and then lead the group to read silently through the liturgy. At the sound of a bell, the first reader begins.

Reader 1:	Button, button who's got the button? Sing a string. Stitch in time. Tie a tale. The button's mine.
Unison:	Button, button who's got the button?
Reader 1:	Weave and womb. Spin a yarn. Fashion worlds with wit and charm.
Unison:	Button, button who's got the button?
Reader 1:	Button up left. Button down right. Gender and class get buttoned too tight.
Unison:	Button, button who's got the button?
Reader 1:	Button or not button? Undress or repress? Stress will unravel all manner of dress.
Unison:	Button, button who's got the button?

Reader 1:   So —
                sing a string.
                Stitch in time.
                Tie a tale.
                Secure the line.
                Button, button
                who's got the button?

Unison: We do
                and
                we will
                and
                we
                can.

One person from each group comes to pick up a bowl or basket of buttons and takes it back to her group. She starts the basket of buttons around the circle, asking each to select a button. When the circle is complete, she explains briefly why she selected her button and invites the group to each share their choice (five to seven minutes). When all have shared, the bell rings again.

Reader 1:   Button, button
                who's got the button?

                Sing a string.
                Stitch in time.
                Tie a tale.
                The button's mine.

Unison: Button, button
                who's got the button?

Reader 1:   Weave and womb.
                Spin a yarn.
                Fashion a world
                with wit and charm.

Unison: Button, button
     who's got the button?

A second person comes to the center and selects enough strands of yarn, each threaded with a big needle, for each member of her group. A musical interlude follows. That second person returns to the group and gives each member a strand with a needle to use to thread the button. The reader begins after they are seated and the bell rings.

Reader 2: **First Lesson in Her-story of Buttons**
    Button: Usually a disk-like piece of solid material having holes or a shank through which it is sewed to one side of an article of clothing and used to fasten or close the garment by passing through a loop or hole in the other side. Purely decorative, non-utilitarian buttons are also frequently used on clothing.

The Questioner asks the following questions once, and then repeats the list, with pauses in between so that women in each group can share their responses to the questions.

Questioner: If a button is for holding things together,
    what is mine holding?

    If a button is for bringing the other side close,
    what is the other? How close is close?

    Why does a button, a solid form with holes, feel so familiar, so foreign to me?

    Does passing through loopholes seem to be a daily practice in my life of work and worship?

The women each take a few minutes to share whatever the button means now to them as the others thread their buttons onto the yarn, tie the ends, and remove the needle. After everyone shares conversation, the Questioner invites all to this unison prayer:

Unison: Holy One, fasten me securely for the ins and outs of life.

Questioner: Genesis 3:1–21 (Hebrew Scripture)

The Questioner follows the same procedure of asking the questions once, then again, slowly, with separation time between each question for response.

Questioner: Is my story of human clothing a matter of shame, a fashion of concealment?

Do I have garments of suffering, glad rags of hope?

Who assists me in "altar-ing" repression into garments of expression?

The group leader invites each person to "put on" her button necklace. When all have done this, the second reader invites prayer by lining out the following and asking all to repeat after her:

Unison: Holy One, clothe me in a holy/human fashion, designed to be form-fitting and free.

Reader 1:   **Next Lesson in Her-story of Buttons**
The ancient Greeks and Etruscans fastened their tunics at the shoulders with buttons and loops. Prior to buttons, garments were laced together or fastened with brooches or clasps and points. Buttonholes were invented in the thirteenth century. Commonly used material for buttons were bone and wood. By the fourteenth century in Europe, buttons became so prominent that in some places laws were passed putting limits on their use. The wearing of gold, silver, and ivory buttons was an indication of wealth. Buttons were now considered ornaments and were placed from elbow to wrist and from neckline to waist.

Follow the same pattern as before, but the groups are asked to open their circles and form a larger group. Provide a music interlude if the group is large. A bell sounds and the Questioner begins. This time any one in any group is encouraged to speak in response to the questions.

Questioner: What might hold the world together if buttons were outlawed?

Are race, gender, class, age, culture, region, and health buttons that I push or use to connect different sides or styles or selves?

What sort of person or community invented button-holes?

The sharing continues. After several minutes, the bell sounds and the Questioner invites all into the unison prayer.

Unison: Holy One, teach us to buttonhole as a means of freeing up, not tying down.

Reader 2: **Third Lesson in Her-story of Buttons**
The history of buttons is definitely a study in authority and organization. Their use on uniforms is a special field for collectors. Military buttons, for example, are used to denote rank and regiment. U.S. Air Force uniform buttons with a hidden compass inside were worn by pilots in case they were shot down and needed to find their way on the ground in a strange land. The most specialized collection of uniform buttons is composed of nothing but staff buttons from different British "insane asylums," as they were once called. Buttons were forbidden for patients' uniforms, however. Considered health hazards because of choking or spitting, they offered too many options for a patient's peace of mind.

Reader 1:   Button up left.
             Button down right.
             Gender and class
             get buttoned too tight.

             Button or not button?
             Undress or repress?
             Stress can unravel
             all manner of dress.

Unison: Button, button
             who's got the button?

A Reflection and Group Sharing

As a musical arrangement based on "Blessed Be the Tie That Binds" is played, each member of the group is invited to pick a second button and bring it into the center space and exchange with another and then another until the music ends.

Reader 1:   So —
             sing a string.
             Stitch in time.
             Tie a tale.
             Secure the line.
             Button, button
             who's got the button?

Unison: We do
             and
             we will
             and
             we can!

             Holy One, bind us together.
             Fasten us firmly.
             Fashion us to hold on to justice,
             and buttonhole peace. Let it be so.

> *In second childhood we move into what some have called
> a receptive mode of consciousness — as opposed to an
> action mode — where images and free association within
> space take precedence over temporal, logical thinking,
> with its desire for prediction and control. We become like
> the little child, not in the literal foolishness of pretending
> to be one, but in the graceful wisdom of one who has
> recovered the capacity of wonder and surprise.*[28]
>
> — Urban T. Holmes

*Some women may wish to add their new button to their
necklace and some may wish to keep it separately.*

Doll Makers
integrating childhood images into an object
as a form of self-knowledge and storytelling

Need for ritual: Playing dolls is an activity that integrates
childhood memories and creativity. Making dolls can be
a way to form a community or open new experiences for
a group that has been together a long time. Memory and
imagination become tangible objects that can be shared in a
group as a form of self-knowledge and expression.

Who: Women in a study group or in a shared community.

Where: In any space where there are comfortable chairs and
working tables.

When: The suggested pattern is to begin the doll creation after
lunch, break for supper, and then return for an evening
session. Close the session with a sharing of the answer to
the question "Who is this?" If there's time for a morning
session, longer narratives can be called for. Often women
will take the dolls to sleep with them and have rich stories

to tell in the morning that incorporate dreams and memories that have "returned" to them during the night.

Components:
- ◆ wide range of cloth pieces and yarn
- ◆ buttons, and other sewing notions
- ◆ threaded needles, glue guns, and staplers
  (no sewing machines)

Music: Should be used for the sessions when the dolls are being made. Childhood songs or favorite popular melodies can be played as the women work.

Ritual: The sharing of personal narratives connected to the dolls is the key ingredient. After each sharing, a communal response can be offered such as "And God said, 'Good, very good.'" As each woman shares her story and her doll, she can place it on a table in the center of the room; the ritual can include a blessing of the dolls and doll makers.

Adaptability

These ritual possibilities using commonplace items like buttons, quilts, and dolls can provide the kind of credibility, guiding metaphor, and emotional resonance that is necessary to a life-sustaining community. Women who can reasonably expect to live for nearly a century must have the opportunity to share common experiences as well as incorporate new persons and patterns. The ability to generate community is essential for those whose lives depend on mutuality and dependence. Rituals of recognition offer nurture and support for women who join in them by reinforcing identity and structures of intimacy. The following poem can be used, for example, as a closing blessing for an afternoon of quilting stories or read in a church service where a woman's quilt is used as the altar covering.

THE QUILTERS
by Heather Murray Elkins

Blessed be the tie that binds:
the heart
the kindred mind
the tear
the inward pain
the hope to meet again.

They are-were-always
frontier followers
pioneers in Jesus
Quilters of the Call
gather in
night and noon
scraps of shadows
snippets of light
to gossip for God.

They could-would-always
stitch story to story
skin to skin
quilt with gut-string
to trace the grace
of newly born or freshly wed
the children's children
their treasured dead.

So
armed with simple thimbles
Quilters of the Call
piece
the four-square gospel
crossXstitch
truth in time.

—© 1989, revised 2001

Chapter Four

Going Home

Gathered together in this closing chapter are stories, narratives, rituals, and a theo-poetic essay drawn from the experience of human living and holy dying. Each woman's experience is unique yet infused with wisdom; there are dynamic tensions and tender reconciliation in each. In the midst of great diversity we are offered the conviction of each woman's community that her experience of dying was for them God-directed and Spirit-filled. In the end we simply affirm that we are wisest when we pray, "Into your hands, Holy One, we commit our body-spirit."

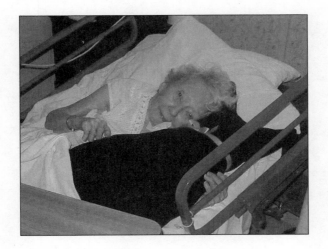

"Let Me Go Home"

SUSAN RAY BEEHLER

…for Adah, a strong woman of faith,
who knew the joy of living and the resurrection in dying
October/November/December 1984

A Serendipitous Dance of Death

MARTHA ANN KIRK

Ada, my mother, loved learning and life. She loved them so much that when she was at the retirement age of sixty-five, she offered to keep teaching high school half-day if they needed and wanted her. With ever creative units on words, poetry, prose, and writing, she became a legend, a living history at the high school. She would welcome a new student: "I remember when I taught your father and he did such a good paper on Huck Finn.... I really enjoyed teaching your grandmother in the one-room schoolhouse with all eight grades."

She wrote of the beauty of the earth and the family land purchased in 1877 as a piece of God's precious creation. In light of her love for nature and for exercise, at seventy-eight she entered the town's first five-kilometer "Wildflower Wellness Run" and got the first-place trophy for a woman over sixty. She said, "I wasn't very fast; it was just that no one else my age would do the race." After all, she had always loved the country roads with spring flowers, and she would briskly walk a few miles most evenings "not to get rusty." That same year, she came with me to the national Sacred Dance Guild Festival and she energetically participated in the liturgical dance workshops. As she explained, the dance was to be a prayer so the technique didn't have to be perfect. She liked to pray so she could just dance any way she wanted to.

In May of her eightieth year, Ada was still enthusiasti-
cally teaching high school English honors classes half-time and
coaching students in dramatic reading for competitions. She retired that summer, but the following year she was still helping
to teach scripture at her church. On Palm Sunday she taught
the mysteries of suffering, death, and new life. She also broke
her wonderful warm homemade cinnamon rolls with the class,
a sweet eucharist that she celebrated so well.

The day after Palm Sunday, she was hospitalized. The doctors
said her heart was blocked — her eighty-one-year-old heart was
blocked. I don't think that it was blocked. I think that her heart
was just bursting from so much love — love for every frustrat-
ing student, love for the lost cousin, love for us even when we
were not so good, love for all God's children as the headlines
proclaimed that our country was starting to bomb Baghdad.
For one month she was confined to a hospital bed, and then
set free.

Earlier she had written, "Serendipity is the wonderful ability
of finding valuable or agreeable things not sought for. . . . If students are aware of the workings of serendipity, the challenges
from high school classes can be ongoing for a lifetime. With un-
quenchable desire, open eyes, and inquiring minds, they will opt
to be intellectually curious about everything under the sun all
the days of their lives. I have discovered the 'found' gold intrin-
sic in striving to stay mentally alert through studying, reading,
and word-watching. And after many years of making magical
discoveries, it is my wish that the students receive this gift and
can say as I do: 'I live a serendipitous life!' "

In both the obituary printed in the newspaper and an invitation sent to the high school and to friends, people were invited
according to Ada's directions to bring "serendipities" to share
at her vigil service.

Ada's mother, who had worked hard on a farm, had taken
time to grow lovely, delicate maidenhair ferns. One of the many
serendipities was the fern that flanked Ada's coffin. Pieces of the

fern were placed on a small memorial card with some of Ada's favorite scripture passages. These were then copied and printed and given to the guests. The image of the fern was a reminder that the beauty and life goes on from generation to generation.

The funeral home was packed. The line was so long out-side they were saying to me, "You should just sell tickets and then you could retire." Finally the funeral director said we just needed to start the vigil service; there was no way to shake everyone's hand and to seat everyone.

I didn't know until that moment if I would have the courage to dance, but she had done the joyful, grateful dance of life and dancing release was the least I could do. I was wearing her deep purple dress, a Mexican flowing cotton gauze dress with shiny purple ribbon. I held the orange and purple silk scarf that I brought her from a market stall near the Church of the Holy

Sepulcher in Jerusalem like a foreshadowing cloth from where they had wrapped Jesus.

My dance began like unfolding wings, and then I cradled arms and hands. The Bible has many images of God as a mother bird hovering over and protecting her little ones. Jesus had compared himself to such a mother as he looked down at Jerusalem. Scripture has another idea of a mother bird. A mother eagle teaches her young to fly by holding it on her back, then beginning to fly, and finally swooping out from under the little bird, coaxing it to fly freely. One would rather ride on the mother forever, but one needs to learn to fly alone.

At first I danced at a distance from the coffin. The deep purple I wore matched the deep purple shrouding her cold body. Finally I had the courage to dance closer, for she wanted to dance through me. As I threw the silk scarf and it floated gently glimmering, she was freer and freer to soar. For one month she had been tied down in bed so that she would not pull out the respirator or tubes with nourishment. We kept telling her we loved her, we wanted her.

Somewhere deep within me was a line from the poet Tagore that she had taught me, "Let my love like sunlight surround you."[29] Our love needed to be transformed from the love that ties down to the sunlight love that warms, that invites more life, that lets one go free. My brother and I, just for an instant, were beginning to learn that sunlight love. In that instant of sunlight love, she could dance, she would soar to what eye has not seen and ear has not heard. I kept dancing.

> The snare of the fowler will never capture you
> and famine will bring you no fear.[30]

I tried to embody the words of the psalmist, "My mourning was turned into dancing" (Ps. 30:11). I could not do a dance of joy, but the power of the resurrection began to stir my body. John the Baptist leapt in Elizabeth's womb when Mary and the unborn Jesus visited. I was learning to leap outside of Ada's womb though it was very hard. I danced reaching out and touching her cold hand. Like Michelangelo's Creator's hand giving spirit to Adam, she was even then filling me with spirit. Yes, the beginning of Genesis speaks of the Ruah, the air, the breath, the wind that hovered over the chaos, bringing forth creation. My life was in chaos. I did not know how to live without a mother. Momma was always here, her womb encircled and nurtured me, her arms cradled me. All were fragments, chaotic clumps, but the Spirit of God hovered over the chaos. The dance continued. Sometimes I hovered, sometimes I was held, sometimes I slumped in sorrow, sometimes I soared in freedom.

In the Middle Ages, when tragedies like the bubonic plague took two-thirds of the population, church people searched for ways to teach one to be prepared. Death dressed as a skeleton came to dance with prince, pauper, and pope, with maiden and monarch. Death personified came to church festivals and invited someone to dance.[31] Both laughter and terror ran through the crowd as this partner appeared. No one wants to dance with her, but the truly wise finally learn as St. Francis did to welcome Sister Death, whom he praises in his Canticle to Brother Sun, Sister Moon, Brother Fire, and Sister Water.

I am beginning to learn some of the rhythm of welcoming Sister Death. Sister Death leads one into the cosmic dance, more splendid and spirited than we can imagine. Ada, whose second name was Sophie, that is, Wisdom, had pasted a card on her study wall: "This is the day the Lord has made. Let us rejoice and be glad in it" (Ps. 118:24). She recognized beauty. Ada invited us to live in joy, hope, gratitude, wonder, generosity, wisdom, and love.

A cousin whose mother had died a few years before wrote a poem to her mother the day after the vigil service.

Oh, Mama, did you see Martha dance last night?
Did you see Jesus smile down on her?

Stroke her long hair
and caress her final step?
Mama, were you there with me
when Martha danced at Jesus' feet?

Dance in the face of death. Living faith is not all about the resurrection of the words; it is about the resurrection of the body. Whatever that is, we don't really know, but dance, for "in my flesh I know that my redeemer lives." I believe in all that is seen and unseen. That is creed enough. Serendipity!

Ada Sophie's Memorial
A Prayer Service with Serendipities

Hymn: "Amazing Grace" by John Newton

Prayer

First Reading: Romans 8:28

"All things work together for good for those who love God." (Repeated three times by an actress cousin who knows how to caress the words.)

Liturgical Dance

By her daughter Martha Ann to the song "Eagle's Wings" by Michael Joncas[32]

Gospel Reading: John 11:21–27

Martha complained to Jesus that her brother Lazarus had died, but then came to believe in Jesus as resurrection and life.

Shared Reflection of Serendipities

Many persons came to the open microphone to share what wonderful surprises they had found through knowing Ada. A young man whom she had taught about seven years before in high school shared that he had not been doing too well, but then Ada quietly confided, "You are my favorite, and I know you will do well." He flourished. Recently as he was confiding this story to his fiancée, he mentioned his teacher's inviting comment. The fiancée replied, "You couldn't have been her favorite, I was. That is what led me." He was wondering how many of us in the room thought we were her favorites and consequently did much more than we ever imagined we could do. The laughter of affirmation swept through the funeral home.

Prayers of Intercession from the Catholic Order of Christian Funerals

The Lord's Prayer

Closing Hymn: "Alleluia! Alleluia!"

Text by Christopher Wordsworth, Music by Ludwig von Beethoven ("Ode to Joy")

Adaptability

This is a vigil service designed by a daughter for her mother that took place the night before the funeral service. The daughter is a dancer and therefore incorporated dance into the service. An older woman could design her own service that others would carry out after her death, or women could participate in helping to design funeral services for other women who have died. These services need to be designed keeping in mind the personality of the particular woman, the elements expected for funeral services in a particular denomination, and the gifts of those who will celebrate the woman's life.

This liturgy included hymns, prayers, scripture reading, liturgical dance, and testimonies by the people present to the life of the woman who died.

As you begin to contemplate writing your own funeral service or designing a service for someone else, there are some basic questions to ask:

What were the woman's favorite scripture passages?

What were the woman's favorite hymns or songs?

What poetry or reading or quotation would reflect the woman's life?

Who among the woman's family and friends have special gifts to offer during the service? To offer a liturgical dance? To sing a solo? To play a musical instrument?

What is the structure of the funeral service that is most common in the woman's denomination? Can that structure or order be used as a foundation or guideline for this service? What elements of the denomination's service do you want to keep? Which do you want to omit? Can it be personalized by adding favorite texts, songs, readings? How will the service begin? How will it end?

Who will be asked in advance to provide testimony, witness, or story sharing? Or will there be an open time when all those present will be offered a chance to share a short witness related to how the woman touched their life?

18

A Country Way of Dying

HEATHER MURRAY ELKINS

One of the values drawn from Appalachia's tradition of wise women can be described as "paring down to the core." It describes a process of conscious restructuring of self in relationship to the community as one's physical and mental abilities decline. "Paring down" is an organic image, drawn from women's culturally assigned work of cooking. It offers a strong contrast to the current marketing of "super-elders" who can do all things in endless leisure, given the proper medication and financial planning. This Appalachian "paring down" process is historically rooted in an economy and ecology that couldn't afford to throw anything useful away. "Use it up, patch it up, wear it out" was an everyday litany. It shaped the stuff of life for many women. This creative recycling of material things as well as one's self was a source of individual pride and community approval for aging women.[33] This was one of the gifts of aging: adaptability.

Adaptability, the desire to be humanly useful and to maintain the deep familial structures of the community, is part of the mind-set for a generation of women who are now passing on. *Passing on* is a familiar expression in Appalachia for dying. It draws on the image of life and death as a pilgrimage or journey. Holy human living and dying are understood as a process that is organic, natural, connected, and embedded in family and community. Learning to live with dignity within a circle that grows increasingly smaller is part of the wisdom tradition that elders can offer their families and community.

I saw this generalization up close and particular in my mother's mother. We were a three-generation family, not uncommon in Appalachia. As long as Grandma lived, she practiced this "paring down to the core," looking for ways to keep her connections alive as she aged. She worked as a bookkeeper in a laundry, ran a grocery store, and farmed. She was in her sixties when her responsibilities were pared down to the traditional role of homemaker for three generations who lived under one roof.

Over a forty-year period, this seemingly forever old woman continued to demonstrate adaptability and the desire to be humanly useful in a very fluid family context. Food preparation was her central activity, and she used it to provide stability and a sacramental consciousness in an often chaotic context where both parents worked and the residence changed every few years. She provided meals and the means to say grace over time and through space.

When she couldn't cook entire meals for the family any longer, she negotiated her transition by making bread once a week. When that ability was diminished, she began to set the table, a task once assigned to the children. She then limited herself to the silverware when she couldn't handle plates any longer. When her eyesight failed, she'd sit at the kitchen table and stir or chop whatever was needed for whoever was cooking. She worked against the loss by looking for what was left to her, paring down to the core. It was a spiritual discipline, a cultural value that was incorporated, that is, structured into her body and personality and community.

What distinguishes this desire to be humanly useful from a workaholic culture that measures human value exclusively in terms of productivity? Some of the difference is cultural, such as land-based intergenerational families whose labor is not rigidly divided by gender or age. Some distinction can be traced to a long-standing marginalization from mainstream America. Elders paring down their lives in the midst of their family and community were seen as older and wiser models of humanity. Those who had to face separation from the family home, the premature limitation of life skills, and the absence of intergenerational contact were to be pitied, because that was how the "outlanders" lived.

Death is nature's way of saying, your table's waiting.
— Robin Williams

Rites of passage are rituals that mark a change in place, state, social position, or age,[34] but going from feeding to being fed is a gradual change that requires a series of realizations or ritualizations rather than a single rite. Her transition from feeding to being fed was informally negotiated by Grandma and various family members, but the informality of the transition was shaped by the dominant cultural values of what Appalachians would call "country ways." At the heart of the cultural issue is a sacramental question: What makes a human being capable of being grateful or making *eucharistia?* Who teaches us to bless, not bite, the hand that feeds us? What smoothes the transition? Being able to see how it's done, up close, personal.

At the age of 106, my grandma had finally traded places, from feeding to being fed. I've framed her lesson in my memory so I will know how to do it when my time comes. My older sister's kitchen is filled with the noisy sounds and wonderful smells of a multigenerational Thanksgiving dinner. My oldest sister had inherited our grandmother's cooking skills; I inherited the ability to boil water. I did as I was told: feed Grandma. Long after other tastes have departed, the sense of bitter and sweet remains, so Grandma eats desert first. I spoon feed her ice cream, my attention elsewhere, until she stops the spoon. Being blind she traces the spoon to my fingers, and kisses my hand. It's a simple gesture of gratitude and a profound insight on what it means to be a wise woman. To kiss the hand that feeds you is at the heart of life lived as sacrament.

Knowing by Heart

Grandma broke her hip when she was 104, and she stayed with us for several weeks after the surgery. Everyone who helped her she called "Mama." If we were slow in answering her call, she'd change it to a question, "Are there any humans here?" When I'd get her ready at night, I'd start the Lord's Prayer. It was a way of signaling that it was bedtime. It also tested if she was still "there." In her prayer I'd hear the firing of synapses as she combined her recent experience and the oral structures of the Lord's Prayer, Baptist style. When she'd come to the end of the prayer, she'd say, "for ever and ever. . . . " She'd then pause for a moment before continuing with: "Humpty Dumpty sat on a wall, Humpty Dumpty had a great fall. . . . " Her voice would taper off for a moment, and then she'd say, "I don't remember how this prayer ends."

I was hearing her basic vocabulary of prayer, her oldest liturgical texts. Because I'd heard the stories, I knew the name of the woman who had taught her the prayers and the rhymes. Mary was her young cousin who came to help with the new babies in a family of thirteen children. She'd fed and rocked and sung to my grandmother, teaching her the Lord's Prayer and nursery rhymes at the same time. This recognition of the importance of an oral tradition and the realization that the memory-embedded material can be reconstructed in illuminating ways is essential for the work of constructing rituals for this population. What might constitute a "ritual core" for a woman, a family, a community? Those gestures, narratives, texts that are known by heart. The core memories that constitute a personal self can be summoned by a shared recitation of a scripture passage such as Psalm 91, or by singing an old hymn, a song from childhood, or even a nursery rhyme. The shared recitation or song provides a moment of a real re-membering of the self.

Many women clergy have seen this at work in countless pastoral settings, with music as the catalyst for memory and a re-membering of self. In order to ensure that "we attend to such events fully, which is to say, spiritually, psychologically, and socially,"[35] we need an intentional retrieval of a family's or a community's oral tradition in order to share in the memorization and recitation of the songs, poems, and texts that constitute the core experience of members of that community.

Conspiring Song Ritual

Need for ritual: As we age we need to create new systems of nurture that celebrate the holy humanness of life through singing, which is an act of breathing, *con-spiring* together).[36]

Setting: Retreat center, church, or home

Participants: Women (small groups of six to eight)

Process: Members are asked to select the one song or hymn that they know by heart and want used at their memorial service. They will need several days to prepare to share the music with the whole group. They are also asked to share a brief story (three to five minutes) explaining "Why this particular song?" Taped music can be used as long as the words are provided so that all can sing. Someone who can accompany each choice should be given the music prior to the ritual. If there are more than eight members of the group, then the ritual should be held twice or two or three women can share once a month until all have been heard.

A common meal is shared followed by the sharing of the stories of the songs and the singing. The explanation of "con-spiring," or breathing together, and its connection to "inspiration" and "spiritus" are made at the start of the presentations. After each woman shares her story about her selection, the hymn or song is sung. Readings and instrumental music can be used to provide breathing room after two or three songs or stories.

Another pattern would begin with the reading and chanting of several psalms, followed by scripture, prayer, and the sharing of the stories and the singing, and then the celebration of the Eucharist. The time frame would be approximately two hours with the meal, the songs, and the stories.

When I'm Down on My Knees

A common core of individual and corporate memory also includes ritual gestures as well as basic body movements that help us to remember as well as prepare us for the time when all memory ceases. Kneeling to pray at the side of a bed before sleeping is a ceremonial gesture that can reconnect and reconstruct the self-conscious memories of the child, the girl, the grown woman, within a woman growing old. Kneeling can be an ambiguous gesture for many women, filled with implications of a forced surrender, but it is also a powerful gesture of trust. It remains a key gesture of faith in many Appalachian faith communities' acts of public worship.

If praying, either privately or publicly, involves articulating the body as well as speaking the unspeakable life of the spirit, then kneeling in prayer at the edge of a bed brings one to the edge of language itself. To be at the edge of a bed in prayer signifies the boundaries between conscious and unconscious; dreams, sleep, sex, birth, illness, secrets, pleasure, pain, and death are all within reach. To kneel side-by-side with another demonstrates a profound commitment to be present to each other in life and in death. To kneel in prayer, either silent or spoken, at the side of a bed when a loved one is sick or dying requires a transparency of purpose, a naked intention. You are in this posture because you are praying.

Many of the now older women I came to know as a pastor in West Virginia would talk about seeing their parents or their grandparents kneel at the edge of a bed and pray together. It was not a practice that they themselves followed but one that they "treasured" as a memory. It is unclear as to why a gesture so valued would cease being practiced. The following suggested ritual is offered as a possible way to reclaim this practice of bodily prayer.

Teach Us to Pray Ritual

Need for ritual: We hunger to pray together in times and places outside of public worship but lack the knowledge to structure such opportunities. "Teach us to pray" is still an essential request for those who want to be wise.

Setting: In a shared living arrangement such as a retirement community or at a retreat center

Participants: Small groups of women, divided into threes

Process: An evening of study can be offered on forms of prayer (intercession, thanksgiving) including scriptural prayers and prayers from other faith traditions. The women are invited to write down the first prayer they learned or a table grace, or to recite one of the prayers that they know by heart. They are asked to share briefly who taught them how to pray or whom they taught to pray. They are then asked what they want others to pray for them as they prepare to go to sleep. Each woman writes a brief prayer for the other two. After the prayers are completed, the three women will go to the bedside of each member, one by one. They'll kneel together at the side of the bed, join hands, and pray aloud or in silence for the woman who will sleep there. Before rising, they say in union: "Heart of our heart, into your hands we commit our lives. Amen." When each woman retires, the prayers that the others have written for her can be placed under the pillow or on the nightstand.

Down from the Apple Tree

One of the decisions made by family and sometimes the woman herself is to allow death to occur unchallenged. This willingness to "let Death in the front door" or, in the words of an old folk tale, "let Mr. Death down from the tree" is seen as organic, a link between holy human living and dying. This was not an active ending to a life, but a letting be. Food, medicine, and hospitalization are declined unless the pain is unbearable.

It was not uncommon for members of the community to come and "sit a spell" with the person who was dying. Traditional Appalachian culture valued keeping watch with the dying as part of a communal agreement. Neither the family nor the one dying was left alone, although there were some distinct disadvantages if too many people tried to keep watch.[37]

My grandmother's death was a slow unraveling of her life along these traditional lines. She was "to home" as she died, cared for by an extended community.

Her passing came early in the morning, at 2:00 a.m. There hadn't been any signs that she was weaker, but the entire family was awake when it happened. She simply stopped breathing. Calls were made to the extended family. (I was in church in South Korea, preparing to preach, when the news came.)

The Appalachian roots of the family tree were revealed in what happened after she died. The body was left as she'd died, resting on its side, hands clasped as if in prayer. One clock in the house was stopped. Everyone waited until Brucie, the favorite granddaughter, could get there by car, a matter of six or seven hours. She washed her body, changed the gown, and fixed her hair. The family helped make up a clean bed and picked out the dress to give the undertaker. Several items, a favorite blanket and a toy lamb, were selected to be buried under an apple tree out in the field. After all that was finished, they called the funeral home. Their quiet acceptance of the family's process was all part of a country way of dying.

19

Now I Lay Me Down to Sleep

KATHY BLACK

It was the year 1920, and "Susan" was the name on the birth certificate. But it didn't really identify this new baby since the doctor wrote in the name "Susan" for any baby girl born in that hospital.

Susan grew up in a large farm family in the south. She was raised in the Southern Baptist Church and encouraged to go to college. Even as a young college student, Susan was always concerned about others — especially children. During her college years she started a breakfast program for poor kids in schools, beginning decades of service to her community, her future family, her country, and her God. In many ways, she was a professional woman ahead of her time who seldom worked for pay but was constantly offering her gifts and skills to help others.

She eventually married and had three children. Wherever they lived, she was actively involved with her church (Methodist now), with the League of Women Voters, the needs of her neighbors, and the political campaigns of people she believed in. She taught cooking and housekeeping to runaway youth, started a summer program for underprivileged kids, supported refugee resettlement for those escaping the horrors of war in Central America as part of the Sanctuary movement, supported children in El Salvador, served on various church committees, was a youth group leader at one church, started a clothes closet and tutoring program at another church, served on city and state commissions, worked on population issues, and in general provided a safe place for children and youth alike. She had a passion for her family, a passion for justice, and a passion for helping others. She was seldom at rest, juggling many volunteer jobs simultaneously. She had a deep and abiding faith that was the foundation of her various ministries, her love of others as children of God, and her constant work for peace and justice in our world.

Her family was very close, and despite the transitions of marriages and moves and the birth of grandchildren, they continued to be a tightly knit family. After celebrating her fiftieth wedding anniversary, when Susan was seventy-four, she knew changes were happening within her body, but she was a very private person and didn't want her family to worry, so she didn't tell anyone. Her children thought she might be drinking too much because they noticed her speech was slurred — most often in the evenings after a glass of wine or two at dinner. Susan, however, was beginning to think she had a brain tumor. She was stumbling a little and controlling her hand while writing was becoming an issue. She became more reticent and withdrawn, feeling scared, not knowing what was happening and why. She finally told her husband and children and went to a large research hospital for testing. While the symptoms persisted and got worse, the tests revealed nothing concrete for two years. She was now falling over backward without warning, losing peripheral vision, and having great difficulty in speaking and writing. Susan was eventually diagnosed with progressive supranuclear palsy.

Progressive supranuclear palsy, or PSP, is a terminal neurological disease of indignity that renders the body a vegetable but does not touch the clarity of the mind until the end when some forms of dementia may be involved. There is no cure. The person (personality, mind, emotions, psyche) becomes locked in a body that cannot respond. Eventually the face becomes rigid so few emotions (pain, distress, joy) can be expressed. The person's intellect and brain functioning remain intact, but because the communication center deteriorates, the body does not respond to the mind's signals so that speech, writing, and walking become impossible even though one is telling the body to do these things. It becomes extremely difficult to swallow, often resulting in choking (one cause of death in PSP patients), and stomach tubes for feeding are recommended to prolong life.

> *The invisible part of me is not old. In aging we gain as well as lose — our spiritual forces expand. A life of the heart and mind takes over as our physical force ebbs away.* —A ninety-year-old-woman

Within four years, this extremely active, caring woman needed help to stand, move, go to the bathroom, and eat. She could no longer teach, speak at meetings, register people to vote, or have extended conversations with her friends and family. Her intellect and passion were fully intact, but she could not communicate except by short words and code phrases, emphasizing her message with gestures, a faint smile, a nod. She lost all privacy and control over her body and her life. Eventually she had to have aides by her side twenty-four hours a day, seven days a week.

In many ways Susan responded in classic fashion. At first she denied that anything was wrong; then she was angry at the situation and at God. She felt like God was punishing her. Before she received a concrete diagnosis, she let her church family know that she was angry at God and didn't understand why this was happening to her. Her faith was faltering and emotions moved back and forth between grief and anger.

A doctor they went to for help in balancing her medications identified her spiritual struggle and recommended that the family seek spiritual guidance. So they called their pastor, who began visiting every Sunday afternoon. In these "Sundays with

Susan" the two of them discovered that Susan was struggling with questions that were leading her into depths where there are no words, only silence. Losing her ability to speak was one thing, but this was something else. Together, they would sit in silence, and then the pastor would articulate some questions, which Susan could answer with yes or no by squeezing the pastor's hand. Sheer grace led to the formation of each question as the two were discovering that God was indeed present in the midst of this turmoil and suffering. The pastor's constant and abiding presence in the home on weekends when other family members were often present offered support for Susan and the family as they negotiated the hard decisions and prepared the way for a final ritual at home, where the space was already filled with memories of care and conversation for this journey. It was also a way for her church family to be included. The pastor recommended short visits with time to simply be silent with Susan, hold her hand, and tell her they didn't have words for this struggle either, but they loved her.

The last four years of constant decline, pain, falls, inability to communicate clearly, and loss of muscle control were agony in many ways for everyone involved. It was devastating for her husband to see Susan decline so quickly, and there was nothing he could do to stop it. The children wanted to stop this from happening to her, and at first accepting the disease seemed to mean giving up hope. But after acceptance of the disease, their hope became focused on a good death with dignity. They wanted to honor her wish for celebration and to give her all the love they had while she was still with them. They wanted her to truly know, feel, and breathe in all the love around her. Susan was clear that she did not want a feeding tube and did not want her life prolonged. At this point in the process of making decisions, some people choose to write up a living will. But Susan and her husband began investigating other options as well. They contacted a group in Oregon called Compassion in Dying, which provided counseling for them.

After much research and investigation, Susan decided that she wanted to choose the time to die. She wanted to be able to say when simply keeping her alive was not enough. She also wanted a death with dignity and some measure of control and choice in her final days. She knew it was just a matter of time. She would never get better, for it was a degenerative disease. She was just in a waiting period until she couldn't swallow anymore, until she couldn't communicate at all, until, perhaps, dementia set in. She had decided she wanted to die, but she did not want anyone in her family to suffer — emotionally, spiritually, or legally.

Susan talked over the situation with her husband and her pastor and then called her children together (the grandchildren were not involved and have still not been told). She wanted to be sure her children understood how serious she was. Since she was not able to communicate as easily as before, she asked her pastor to tell the children what she wanted — that she wanted to die. Through gestures and simple, short words, squeezing of the hand, Susan communicated clearly enough and confirmed for her family what the pastor said. Susan wanted to know if it was okay with them. Choosing to die is never an easy choice nor is accepting this decision from someone you love dearly. It may be less complicated in states where it is legal, but in states where it is illegal, it carries other implications. The family members and pastor came together several times over the next two months to talk openly about Susan's decision. Susan was clear that she would not act on this decision until all in her family were okay with it.

Susan's family came together to support Susan's decision, bringing her a sense of peace. Susan could choose *how* it would happen and, taking into consideration all the preparations, she could also choose *when* it would happen. Now that she knew she had a choice and the children were okay with her decision, worry and anxiety about her future were put aside. She could now begin to celebrate her life and prepare for her last days. Susan made a list of things she wanted to do to celebrate her life — return to places she adored (the beach, art museums), eat favorite foods brought in from favorite restaurants, get her hair done for the last time, be pushed in her wheelchair through the park with her grandchildren beside her, and something new in her life — to swim. She went to water therapy twice a week, "swimming" with one daughter one day and another daughter the next day. It was a glorious time when the bond between mother and daughter was strengthened and when Susan's body felt free from rigidity and restriction.

Susan asked her daughters to go through the closets, boxes, and items collected through a lifetime so they would know what everything was, its history, its meaning in the family. This inventory became a journey of learning and love, with her daughters discovering stories, surprises, achievements, losses, and joys. Her daughters collected various photographs, newspaper clippings, letters, and documents, and made scrapbooks of their mother's life. Susan's story was relived and retold with new insights and fresh perspectives. She had reclaimed her God and her faith and had the support of her family and her pastor. Although communication was limited, it was clear to all that she lived out her remaining days with grace and dignity, humor and love.

In the meantime, doctors were contacted and medicines obtained that would provide a peaceful, painless death. The pastor was preparing a ritual of honoring, saying good-bye, and blessing for the final day.

The adult children (except for one spouse who was taking care of all the grandchildren) gathered around Susan in the living room at the appointed time. The pastor led them in a ritual that included Native American elements that honored that part of her ancestry, an opportunity for each in the family to say good-bye, a reading, a prayer, and a blessing (see below for the full ritual). Susan also communicated in whatever way was possible that she loved them all.

After the ritual, Susan went into the bedroom with her family and minister and took all the medications required. Her face took on a vibrancy that had not been seen in years, and a peaceful glow surrounded her. In this state of being between life and death, one sang a song from church and camping days, one held her hand, one cradled her and made her comfortable, one shared a story. It wasn't long before she died. At her time of death, a reading was offered (see below).

The family still gathers on various occasions to honor Susan's life and her choice in death. She was truly a remarkable woman. Susan's sisters had always gathered every year for a "sisters' weekend." Now Susan's daughters have their own "sisters' weekend" and join their aunts for a couple of days at the end of their weekend to honor their mother and sister.

Gathering of Susan's Family

Forming a Sacred Circle (spoken by pastor or other ritual leader)

Our faith reminds us that God is the center of creation, of our lives, of the world. As we gather to share these precious moments with Susan, we seek to make this space a sanctuary for us. Let us seek the wisdom of the four directions that surround us and make the circle sacred.

Let us remember the East. From the East, the direction of the rising sun, we glean wisdom and knowledge through desert silences and humble service. May God enable us to be wise.

Let us remember the South. From the South come guidance and the beginning and end of life. Susan, you are moving South. May we walk this path with you as long as we are permitted, and when you continue on, may your journey be safe and smooth.

Let us remember the West. From the West come purifying waters. May we be grateful for life-giving and sustaining water.

Let us remember the North. From the North come strong winds and gentle breezes. May we feel the breath of the Spirit encouraging us.

If we walked a path in each direction, the sacred paths would form a cross. Returning to the center, we discover the one we claim as the Christ, who calls us and challenges us.[38]

Greeting One Another

This can be a set greeting that is said to each one around the circle, for example: "God's Spirit rests upon you."

Reading

From Anne Cameron, *Daughters of Copper Woman* (Vancouver, B.C.: Press Gang Publishers, 1981), 52–54.

Saying Good-Bye

We burned some sage and each family member shared a brief word with Susan, holding the burning sweet grass or sage as a way to let our words go with her.

Concluding Prayer

God of love, we thank you for all with which you have blessed us even to this day: for the gift of joy in days of health and strength, and for the gifts of your abiding presence and promise in the days of pain and grief. We praise you for each person in this family circle, and for all the friends who have expanded the circle over the years. We offer special thanks for Susan, who has made sure that her daughters would know the meaning of "home," and for her faithful witness to each one as wife, mother, mother-in-law, grandmother, great-grandmother, friend. Amen.[39]

Blessing

With her loom and with her broom
with her love and with her patience
she weaves the pattern of destiny
she sweeps beaches and minds
she weaves the pattern of reality
she tidies shorelines and souls.
She will never abandon you.[40]

Reading: The Legend of the Coming of Death from the Code of Handsome Lake, a Seneca Prophet

At the moment of death, "The Legend of the Coming of Death" was read:

When the world was first made, human beings did not know that they must die sometime. In those days everyone was happy and neither men, women, nor children were afraid of anything. They did not think of anything but doing what pleased them. At one time, in those days, a prominent man was found on the grass. He was limp and had no breath. He did not breathe. The human beings that saw him did not know what had happened. The man was not asleep because he did not awaken. When they placed him on his feet he fell like a tanned skin. He was limp. They tried many days to make him stand but he would not. After a number of days he became offensive.

A female said that the man must be wrapped up and put into the limbs of a tree. So the men did so, and after a while the flesh dropped from the bones and some dried on. No one knew what had happened to cause such a thing.

Soon afterward a child was found in the same condition. It had no breath. It could not stand. It was not asleep, so they said. The human beings thought it was strange that a girl should act this wise. So she was laid in a tree. Now many others did these things and no one knew why. No one thought that it would happen to them.

There was one wise person who thought much about these things, and she had a dream. When she slept the Good Minded Spirit came to her and spoke. She slept a long time but the other human beings noticed that she breathed slowly. Now after a time this person rose up and her face was very solemn. She called the people together in a council and addressed them. The people all sat around in a sacred circle.

The wise person spoke and said, "The Good Minded Spirit made every good thing and prepared the earth for human beings. Now it appears that strange events have happened. A good word has come to me from the Good Minded Spirit. The Good Minded Spirit says that every person must do as you have seen the other persons do. They have died. They do not breathe. It will be the same with all of you. Your minds are strong. The Good Spirit made them that way so that you could endure everything that happened. So then do not be downcast when I tell you that you all must die. Listen further to what I say. The name of the one that takes away your breath is S'hondowêk'owa. We do not know what he looks like, and I was not told why this happens just as I do not know how it came to be that we were born.

"You must now divide yourself into nine bands, five to sit on one side of the fire and four on the other, and each band shall care for its members. You must seek out all good things and instruct one another and those who do good things will see when they die the place where the Maker of All Things lives."[41]

Adaptability

A ritual like this is very specific to the person who is dying. The pastor spent endless hours, week after week, with the woman and with her husband and daughters. She knew this woman, her history, her likes and dislikes, her desires. The pastor knew the contributions she had made to the world, her passions and hopes for the future of the world. She also had a pastoral sense of what the family needed at this crucial time in their lives. Out of this deep knowing, the minister designed this ritual.

This is not a ritual that is easily adaptable to another context. However, it can give clues for designing a similar ritual for a specific person in a specific context.

General Guidelines

This type of ritual should only be celebrated after much conversation and prayerful consideration on the part of the woman, the family members involved, and the pastor. Pastoral care through ritual is caregiving only when all want the same thing. If the woman wanted it but the family members didn't, what would have been pastoral for the woman could have been deeply hurtful and faith-challenging to the family.

General ideas about what should take place during a ritual designed for someone near death should be decided by the person (to the degree possible) and by her family. The woman may not be very communicative. The family may be steeped in so much grief that they can't think straight. And neither the woman nor the family members may have any idea how to create a ritual or what to include in it. Some questions to the family may be in order:

What do you want or need to say at this time to your spouse/mother/friend? Are there stories that haven't been shared or words of love and thanks and good-bye that still need to be said or need to be said one last time?

What readings (scripture, quotations, poetry) would be comforting in her last hour?

What music or songs might evoke memories and pleasure?

What prayer language might dwell within so that peace may abide and God's presence be felt during the journey of crossing over?

How should the various elements be ordered?

How will the group gather? Informally or with some formal greeting? In this ritual the greeting was "May God's Spirit rest upon you."

What opening words will be used? An opening prayer, a song or reading of some sort? Or will the family begin immediately with sharing their stories and saying their words of love, thanks, and good-bye?

What symbols will be present? Candles, incense, photos, a favorite quilt, a stuffed animal from a grandchild? What will the room look like? What meaningful elements of the woman's life will be visually present for this moment?

Who will give the blessing (if any)? From family members to the woman and/or (if the woman is capable in some form) from the woman to the family members?

How will the ritual end? With a prayer? A benediction? Passing of the Peace to the woman and to each other?

20

"Daybreak"

MARY ELIZABETH MULLINO MOORE

For Mother

*My Mother (Elizabeth) trusted that each day was new,
and she faced her death as yet another new day,
to be lived fully.*

Daybreak is ever new, as darkness turns to day,
As sunlight spreads across the earth with ever-widening rays.
One day has closed its eyes, and nighttime rest is done,
And day is dawning in God's way, and life continues on.

Each day of life is fresh, and touched by God's own hand.
The whisper of God's Spirit blows in every grain of sand.
For humankind, the dawn proclaims life without end,
But we are challenged day by day to walk with God our Friend.

Daybreak is ever new, for creatures great and small —
A fresh occasion for response to God's persistent call.
The moments come each day to grow in grace from heav'n —
To be the image of our God, and nature's sacred leav'n.

When life is o'er for now, we praise the God of old
For birthing every precious life to dwell within God's soul.
The end of life is blessed, and graced with peaceful rest,
Transformed to glory without end, as blessing and as blest.[42]

—Tune of "Soldiers of Christ Arise"

21

Facing Finitude
Between "Now" and the
"Hour of Our Death"[43]

TERESA BERGER

"Remember, you are dust, and to dust you will return." These stark words traditionally accompany the imposition of ashes on Ash Wednesday.[44] The Lenten reminder of human mortality issues a profound challenge for us to face our own finitude. For centuries, all who came forward at the beginning of Lent to receive ashes were addressed with these words: the young and the old, those in good health and those who were dying, those who unbeknownst to anyone would die within the year and those who had a long life ahead of them. Contemplating death, then, was seen not as a task for the last few moments of life, but rather as an ongoing, lifelong challenge — something to practice from "now" until the "hour of our death."

By contrast, the culture we inhabit labors to avoid such intimate reflection on death, especially our own. As avid consumers of all things material, including life itself, we are supposed to have infinite appetites, and infinite capacity to satisfy these appetites. The burgeoning cultural interest (not least of all commercial) in the "silver" or "golden" years rarely focuses on the existential limit of these years. More surprising than the cultural evasion of dying, however, is that contemporary spiritual practices also offer us few opportunities to confront our own end. Who dares to remind us that we are dust and that to dust we will return?

The knowledge of our own end is not something we can ever really forget. Life is fragile. It takes something as ordinary as a drunk driver to bring on that defining moment of our life. But beyond this deep-seated even if hushed knowledge of the certainty of our own coming death, there is also the possibility of engaging that death deliberately, with open eyes and an open heart. This is a daunting task in our culture. Reflecting upon death can easily be seen as morbid or as a condition needing medical attention (recurring thoughts of death, of course, are one of the symptoms of depression) or as an invitation for the thanatologically sensitive expert to advise us on how to "have a nice death."[45] In what follows, I hope to show that it is precisely the contemporary labored and fleeting experiences with finitude that are distinctly odd, not the faith-filled acknowledgment that one's life is finite. If nothing else, the avoidance of this reflection is doomed to fail in each and all of our lives. And what can be odder than ignoring such a large-scale failure?

Historically, the church has been a place where people learned and practiced together "the art of dying." Even if the medieval practices that constituted this art cannot simply be reclaimed (as if nothing in the world had changed), the Christian faith still offers spiritual wisdom for anticipating death. For many centuries, preparing for death was an important part of the spiritual life. It was something one learned early on, practiced, and taught to children and grandchildren. I seek to befriend this tradition of deliberately anticipating the hour of my death. What resources do we have for this task?

Facing the Scriptures

The scriptures are a good place to begin. They are no strangers to facing finitude and in fact encourage us to do precisely that. The psalmist prays: "Lord, let me know my end, and what is the measure of my days; let me know how fleeting my life is"

(Ps. 39:4). For the psalmist, acknowledging mortality engenders not a morbid fascination with death, but rather wisdom for the living of our days: "Teach us to count our days that we may gain a wise heart" (Ps. 90:12). Jesus tells the parable of a man who lacked precisely such wisdom. This "rich fool" has ably planned ahead for his own estate, all the while ignoring the finite state of his own life. He says to himself, "Soul, you have ample goods laid up for many years; relax, eat, drink, be merry." God's response is simple: "You fool! This very night your life is being demanded of you" (Luke 12:19–20). In a similar vein, the writer of the Letter of James has this frank reminder for his readers:

> Come now, you who say, "Today or tomorrow we will go to such and such a town and spend a year there, doing business and making money." Yet you do not even know what tomorrow will bring. What is your life? For you are a mist that appears for a little while and then vanishes. Instead you ought to say, "If the Lord wishes, we will live and do this or that." (James 4:13–15)

Facing the Light

Facing the Scriptures and their ancient wisdom about the end of life is one way of facing our own end. But the wisdom of the Scriptures meets us not only in texts. We encounter this wisdom also in the biblical stories that have been taken up in the liturgy and popular devotions. A case in point is Luke 2:22–38, the story of Jesus' presentation in the temple and the encounter with Simeon and Anna. The Feast of the Presentation of the Lord celebrates these events annually on February 2. At the heart of this feast stands an encounter: God's own new life, in the form of the infant Jesus, dawns on a man and a woman of advanced age, the two prophets Simeon and Anna. God had told Simeon that he would not see death without having seen the Messiah; Anna was eighty-four years old and clearly coming to the end of her life. When they encountered the infant Jesus, both Simeon and Anna understood that their hour had come. Cradling the infant in his arms, Simeon praised God for letting him depart in peace, since the promise that had kept him alive was fulfilled. He had, indeed, seen the light (Luke 2:32).

This encounter between God's own new life and two elderly people gave rise to a particular devotional practice. On February 2, candles were (and in many places still are) blessed in memory of Simeon and Anna seeing the light. The traditional name for the feast witnesses to this custom: Candlemas. There was also a link between this celebration of Candlemas and the hours of death. The devout would keep at home some of the candles blessed on February 2 to light when someone was dying. It is interesting that in our own times, although a bewildering variety of candles is available "for all occasions," dying does not seem to be a part of this "all." Even in traditional Catholic contexts, we are hard-pressed to find mention of blessed candles for the dying.[46] Emergency telephone numbers for medical personnel, living wills, and directives for private bank accounts concern us profoundly, not religious symbols for the hour of death. But why choose between these different practices? They are in no way exclusionary. Blessing candles on Candlemas for those who will encounter their own death within the year in no way precludes having emergency telephone numbers and living wills ready.[47]

Facing the Night

Within the rhythm of liturgical time, Simeon's response to seeing the light (Luke 2:29–32) appears not only at the Feast of the Presentation of the Lord. These words also have their place in the daily rhythm of prayer since they form the gospel canticle appointed for Night Prayer. We can see this Night Prayer, or Compline (i.e., that which completes the day), as one precious moment, each day, of contemplating death. Written deep into this prayer is the fusion of two horizons, namely, the coming of the night and the coming of our death. As we confront the closure of the day and our own falling asleep, the horizon opens to our last falling asleep from which there will be no awakening to this earthly life. Simeon's song, "Lord, now you let your servant go in peace," is one moment in this liturgical fusion. The concluding Compline prayer also fuses these two horizons: "May the all-powerful Lord grant us a restful night and a peaceful death." If nothing else, making this our prayer every night is one profound way of remembering our own mortality.

Facing the Hour

If facing the night offers a daily reminder of our existential limit, such a moment is also embedded in one of the most traditional and beloved prayers of all times. This prayer is not bound to any specific period, date, place, posture, or need. Millions have prayed it and continue to pray it every day. Whenever this prayer is breathed, it brings the one who prays into direct address with her own mortality: "Holy Mary, Mother of God, pray for us sinners, now and at the hour of our death." What would it look like to make such moments of prayer more explicit? A prayer group I was a part of many years ago dedicated the last prayer "for the one among us who next will have to confront the hour of death." Initially, this prayer startled and unsettled me. Much later, however, a woman in my faith community was killed in a car accident as she drove home from Sunday Mass. I wished then that we had dared to include such an intercession in our public prayers. Our shock and struggle with this sudden death would have had a different dimension, namely, the consolation that we had prayed for this woman just minutes before she got into her car.

Engaging with death in prayer, especially as we become increasingly aware of the fragility of all life, daunts us. The knowledge that this can be done with more than words might offer solace here. Many Christians have turned to music. The chorales of Johann Sebastian Bach that focus on dying and death are a striking example.[48] The well-known passion hymn "O Sacred Head, Now Wounded" begins with a meditation on Jesus' dying agony and ends with a prayer for one's own death. The words, unfortunately, rarely appear in contemporary hymnals, but they are worth committing to memory: "My Savior, be Thou near me when death is at my door; Then let Thy presence cheer me, forsake me nevermore!"[49] I could mention many other chorales and hymns here, but they share the underlying conviction that our meditations upon death might need more than words alone.

Facing Finite Others

Even if I am the only one who will experience that particular death which is mine to die, all of us confront the end. But none of us is alone with this challenge. The Christian tradition offers what we might call "finite others" as companions for this journey. Some of these companions have already been mentioned: biblical authors, the psalmist, Jesus, Simeon and Anna, and the writers of beloved prayers and hymns. There are many more. The saints and all those who lived and died in exemplary ways are one example. Stories of their dying can still inspire, even if their deaths do not take the traditional form of martyrs' stories or edifying deathbed narratives. Think, for example, of the profoundly "obscure" death of Edith Stein, also known as Sister Teresia Benedicta a Cruce. This Jewish philosopher-turned-Carmelite nun died in the gas chambers of Auschwitz. No one knows exactly when and how. The train that brought Edith Stein to Auschwitz arrived on August 9, 1942. There is no trace of her after that, but like countless others, she likely died with her body reduced to smoke and ash. The last eyewitnesses who saw Sr. Teresia alive, however, and scraps of paper written by her in transit to Auschwitz, reveal a woman who faced her own murder without blinking. Sustained by prayer, Sr. Teresia entered a profound solidarity-to-death with her own Jewish people. At the same time, she quietly and resolutely cared for others in the transit camps, especially the children. She washed and cleaned, combed and fed, all the while knowingly walking toward her death. Edith Stein offers us a richly textured life to ponder (she was one of the first women to receive a doctorate in philosophy), but the last days of her life inspire, even as the hour of her death is shrouded in genocidal gas and smoke.

In the communion of saints, there are many, like Edith Stein, with the gift of accompanying the dying. There are saints to aid us with a "good death," among them Birgitta of Sweden and Barbara. The latter especially is traditionally invoked against a "sudden death," that is, a death that finds the person unprepared. None of these saints is in great demand today, especially not the ones invoked against a sudden death. Most people seem to want precisely this kind of death: quick, painless, and, if possible, while asleep, that is, without having to know the dying. Can the patron saints for the dying nevertheless proffer wisdom for today? We may actually need them more than ever, even if not so much for fear of a sudden death. In a culture where most of us will die alone, in hospitals and nursing homes, we may welcome saints who accompany us into the hour of our death when few others will. Maybe these saints can also become companions as we contemplate death throughout our lives. They might enable us to (re-)conceive of our dying as something we need never do entirely alone.

Other companions for this open-eyed journey are those from among our own family and friends who have died. We do well to remember these dearly departed and to offer them continuing hospitality in our midst. Such hospitality can take many forms. Why not, on the anniversary of a death, place a photo of that family member on the kitchen table and light a candle? Children grasp these simple symbols instinctively. The photo and lit candle often prompt the stories we tell about the one who has died but who continues to be a part of our family. Depending on cultural context, hospitality toward the ancestors can take much more elaborate form. The Hispanic celebration of the Day of the Dead, with its home altars full of photos, memorabilia, food, flowers, and candles, is a case in point.

It is not only the familiar dead who are our companions. Indeed our closest companions may well be our living friends and relatives. As we age together, we face our mortality together. There will be those among us who carry the marks of a terminal illness. There are the elderly, who not only are close to their own death, but who have accompanied others on that road and have wisdom to share. Even our children will ask us out of the blue when we will die and where we want to be buried. We all encounter our own death within the larger web of relationships that constitute our lives. It is well to attend to the ways this web is subject to its own finite limits.

Lastly, accepting our own body as it ages also means befriending a companion on the journey to the hour of death. Whether it is our wrinkles, our increasingly gray hair, or the changing rhythms of our (female) bodies, we do em-body our own finite state. Why not befriend more willingly this finite body? It will, after all, be (with) us at the hour of our death, even if no one else is. Befriending our body that will die raises one last question about finite friends and companions on the journey. Can our own death be befriended, too?

Facing Sister Death

An often-quoted prayer of St. Francis of Assisi names death our "sister" for whom we praise God, together with Brother Sun, Sister Moon, Sister Water, Brother Fire, and other siblings. In this prayer Francis befriends death by including it in the created order, all of which points and ultimately leads to the Creator: "Praised be You, my Lord, through our Sister Bodily

Death. . . . Blessed are those whom death will find in Your most holy will, for the second death shall do them no harm."[50]

Envisioning death as a "sister," however, is only one way in the Christian tradition of naming and confronting the end of life. There are other, more negative ones, from the biblical images of death as the "last enemy" (1 Cor. 15:26) or the "wages of sin" (Rom. 6:23) to the ways we mock death ("Where, O death, is your victory?" 1 Cor. 15:55). The breadth of possibilities suggests that naming death defies an easy either-or choice. Whether we experience death as a "sister" or an "enemy" (or as a sister-turned-enemy for that matter) depends not least of all on when and how we encounter death. Different moments in life will make us see death differently. Someone who has just fallen wildly in love, or birthed a child, or almost completed a book will probably think poorly of having to die. Someone who finds herself alone, having lost her beloved after a long and debilitating disease, might welcome her own death.

Wherever we are in life, confronting death is best done as part of a larger whole, namely, the living of life. It is the vision of this larger whole that gives the Christian approach its particular stamp. Our faith invites us to face our end as part of facing the ultimate source of all life: Godself.

Facing the Source of All Life

This might in fact be the most important gift the Christian tradition offers for those willing to contemplate their own death. Our faith envelops this contemplation within our encounter with the ultimate source of life. We live into our own dying most deeply by each day drawing closer to this source of all life, God. A person of faith, who every day prays the ancient commendation of the soul — "Into your hands I commit my spirit" (Ps. 31:5 NIV) — might not need to do much more in the hour of her death. Jesus himself died with these words on his lips.[51] Our faith arguably was born in that very moment, when the ultimate source of all life, God, faced down finitude in the death and resurrection of Jesus of Nazareth. Our life, including the hour of our death, is in good hands with such a God.

Facing Finitude: A Prayer
by Teresa Berger

Graceful God
Weaver of the Web of Life
Mystery at the Heart of the Universe
Holy Wisdom, Vibrant Spirit

I enter
the space of my own dying,
the holy ground of facing finitude,
my own.
I stand before you with empty hands.
The world of appearances
will fade away.
The performances of authority
and the power of my own life
will lose their defining edge.
I can already sense
the web of my life being unmade.
I stand before you with empty hands.

I pray:
as I face my own dying
as I walk on this holy ground
toward the hour of my death,
become for me, yet again,
Holy Wisdom and Vibrant Spirit,
the Mystery at the heart of my own universe,
the Weaver of the Web of Life, your life within me.

Grant me the grace to hold still
and to sense your Spirit hovering over the troubled waters of
     my soul.
Hold me gently in your arms,
when facing my own dying
brings emptiness and agony.
Teach me to yield to my life's unmaking
but also to discern and fight the evils that might surround it.
Sustain me as I try to live
while walking towards my own death.

And when this holy hour of my death comes,
as it so surely will,
when my life is for ever unmade
in that all-defining moment of my life,
let me knowingly yield to you,
Passionate Weaver of the Web of Life,
that you might re-weave my broken web
into the fullness of life that is your own.[52]

Postlude

HEATHER MURRAY ELKINS

My sisters, if you receive these words and gather up the laws and lessons of Love, being attentive to wisdom and inclining your heart to understanding; yes, if you cry out for insight and raise your voice for revelation, if you seek it like silver and search for it as for hidden treasures; then you will understand what it means to love, fear, and trust the Holy One, our Maker, our redeemer, our sustainer. You will find, my sisters, an awesome knowledge of God.

—Based on Proverbs 2:1–5

Be careful what you pray for. I pray to grow wiser as I grow older. I saw this book, *Wising Up*, as a hopeful outcome of the scholarship and teaching of feminist liturgical studies, but the book quickly became more than a matter of words on a page. Language and life went down to the marrow. Between the prelude and the postlude I learned more about aging and ritual than I wanted to know:

- How to stand in the presence of loved ones who suffer and do nothing but sing.

- How to keep a promise and tell the doctors to remove the respirator and let my father die.

- How to respond to my mother's anguish over a misread chart that ended his life on her birthday.

- How to use legal means as a political protest against our nation's dysfunctional structures of health care and as a personal ritual for channeling anger.

- How to celebrate a sixtieth anniversary when the partner is suddenly missing.
- How to find a new place for my mother to live and someone to keep her company.
- How to commit human ashes to the good earth and plant a new apple tree in an old garden.
- How to make peace among three generations of women.

The first and final insight about wising up is that we can't do it alone. My husband, Bill, reminded me of this lesson on the day I was to meet Kathy for the final editing. I was late, frantically unpacking from the trip from West Virginia and repacking for the week in her family home in the Poconos. I lifted out the Korean urn that had held my father's ashes and lost my grip. It tipped and leftover ashes covered both hands. I froze. The whole journey hit a dead-end. I stood staring at my hands, not able to wipe the paralyzing evidence of mortality out of my mind or off my fingers. Bill took the urn, put it on the ground, and placed my hands on his face. He rubbed the ashes on my hands onto his cheek, his chin, and his forehead while saying, "Don't worry. We're safe. You need to go on."

"In life, in death, in life beyond death, God is with us. We are not alone. Thanks be to God."[53]

Appendix

Sources for
Women, Ritual, and Aging

McEwan, Dorothea, Pat Pinsent, Ianthe Pratt, and Veronica Seddon, eds. *Making Liturgy: Creating Rituals for Worship and Life*. Norwich, U.K.: Canterbury, 2001.

> Chapter 4: "Creating Liturgies for Small Groups," by Veronica Seddon
>
> Chapter 5: "Creating Liturgies for Large Groups," by Ann Farr
>
> Chapter 25: " 'Croning': Celebrating a Seventieth Birthday"
>
> Chapter 26: "Menstruation and Menopause"

Neu, Dianne. *Women's Rites: Feminist Liturgies for Life's Journey*. Cleveland: Pilgrim Press, 2003.

> "Designing Feminist Liturgies for Women's Life Passages," p. 41
>
> "Change of Life: Journey through Menopause," p. 160
>
> "Choosing Wisdom: A Croning Ceremony," p. 171

Orenstein, Debra. *Lifecycles: Jewish Women on Life Passages and Personal Milestones*. Vol. 1. Woodstock, Vt.: Jewish Lights Publications, 1994.

> Chapter 14: "Honor Thy Mother: Continuity and Change in the Lives of Aging Jewish Women," by Dena Shenk
>
>> "Responsum: A Voice from an Older Generation," by Mildred Seltzer
>>
>> "Growing Old — My View," by Harriet M. Perl
>>
>> "Widowhood after a Long Marriage: Two Poems," by Barbara D. Holender
>>
>> "A Ceremony of Passage on My Sixty-Fifth Birthday," by Barbara D. Holender
>
> Chapter 15: "A Cosmology of Mourning," by Margaret Fiolub
>
>> "A Modern Version of the Traditional Confessional before Dying," by Vickie Hollander
>>
>> "Suite on My Mother's Death," by Carol V. Devis
>
> "Afterword: How to Create a Ritual," by Debra Orenstein

Ruether, Rosemary Radford. *Women-Church*. San Francisco: Harper and
      Row, 1985.

>   "Menopause Liturgy," p. 204
>   "Croning Liturgy," p. 206
>   "The Dying Vigil," p. 209

Sears, Marge. *Life-Cycle Celebrations for Women*. Mystic, Conn.: Twenty-
      Third Publications, 1989.

>   "Celebration at the Onset of Menopause," p. 22
>   "Comfort Ritual for an Impending Death," p. 25
>   "Celebration of a Wise Woman: 60th to 75th Birthdays, Retirement,"
>   p. 47

St. Aubyn, Lorna. *Everyday Rituals and Ceremonies*. London: Judy Piatkus
      Publishers, 1994.

>   "Menopause," p. 59
>   "Retirement," p. 69
>   "Death 1," p. 73
>   "Death 2," p. 77

Resources on Feminist Liturgy

Adelman, Penina V. *Miriam's Well: Rituals for Jewish Women around the
      Year*. 2nd ed. New York: Biblio, 1990.

Berger, Teresa. *Women's Ways of Worship: Gender Analysis and Liturgical
      History*. Collegeville, Minn.: Liturgical Press, 1999.

Berger, Teresa, ed. *Dissident Daughters: Feminist Liturgies in Global
      Context*. Louisville: Westminster John Knox Press, 2001.

Caron, Charlotte. *To Make and Make Again: Feminist Ritual Thealogy*. New
      York: Crossroad, 1993.

Duck, Ruth C. *Circles of Care: Hymns and Songs*. Cleveland: Pilgrim Press,
      1998.

————. *Finding Words for Worship*. Louisville: Westminster John Knox
      Press, 1995.

Duck, Ruth C., and Patricia Wilson-Kastner. *Praising God: The Trinity in
      Christian Worship*. Louisville: Westminster John Knox Press, 1999.

Elkins, Heather Murray. *Worshiping Women: Reforming God's People for
      Praise*. Nashville: Abingdon Press, 1994.

Henderson, J. Frank. *Remembering the Women: Women's Stories from
      Scripture for Sundays and Festivals*. Chicago: Liturgy Training Publi-
      cations, 1999.

Kirk, Martha Ann. *Celebrations of Biblical Women's Stories: Tears, Milk,
      and Honey*. London: Sheed and Ward, 1987.

Litzinger, Sandra Louise. *Word, Wisdom, and Worship: WomanChurch
      Celebrates the Seasons*. Boulder, Colo.: WovenWord Press, 1999.

Neu, Dianne, and Mary Hunt. *WomanChurch Sourcebook.* Silver Spring, Md.: WATERworks, 1993.

Northup, Lesley A., ed. *Women and Religious Ritual.* Washington, D.C.: Pastoral Press, 1993.

Procter-Smith, Marjorie. *In Her Own Rite.* Nashville: Abingdon Press, 1990.

————. *Praying with Our Eyes Open.* Nashville: Abingdon Press, 1995.

Ricciuti, Gail Anderson, and Rosemary Catalano Mitchell. *Birthings and Blessings: Liberating Worship Services for the Inclusive Church.* New York: Crossroad, 1991.

————. *Birthings and Blessings: More Liberating Worship Services for the Inclusive Church.* Vol. 2. New York: Crossroad, 1993.

Rothschild, Sylvia, and Sybil Sheridan. *Taking up the Timbrel: The Challenge of Creating Jewish Ritual Today.* London: SCM Press, 2000.

Sered, Susan Starr. *Women as Ritual Experts: The Religious Lives of Elderly Jewish Women in Jerusalem.* New York: Oxford University Press, 1992.

Walton, Janet Roland. *Feminist Liturgy: A Matter of Justice.* Collegeville, Minn.: Liturgical Press, 2000.

Walton, Janet Roland, and Marjorie Procter-Smith. *Women at Worship: Interpretations of North American Diversity.* Louisville: Westminster John Knox Press, 1993.

Ward, Hannah, Jennifer Wild, and Janet Morley, eds. *Celebrating Women.* New ed. London: SPCK, 1995.

Wasserfall, Rahel R. *Women and Water: Menstruation in Jewish Life and Law.* Hanover, N.H.: University Press of New England for Brandeis University Press, 1999.

White, Susan J. *A History of Women in Christian Worship.* Cleveland: Pilgrim Press, 2003.

Winters, Miriam Therese. *WomanWord: Women of the New Testament.* New York: Crossroad, 1990.

————. *WomanWisdom: Women of the Hebrew Scriptures.* Part 1. New York: Crossroad, 1991.

————. *WomanWitness: Women of the Hebrew Scriptures.* Part 2. New York: Crossroad, 1992.

Wootton, Janet. *Introducing a Practical Feminist Theology of Worship.* Cleveland: Pilgrim Press, 2000.

Resources on Women and Aging

Black, Helen K., and Robert L. Rubinstein. *Old Souls: Aged Women, Poverty, and the Experience of God.* Hawthorne, N.Y.: Aldine de Gruyter, 2000.

Brice, Carleen. *Age Ain't Nothing but a Number: Black Women Explore Midlife.* Boston: Beacon Press, 2003.

Coyle, Jean M. *Handbook on Women and Aging.* Westport, Conn.: Greenwood Press, 1997.

Cruikshank, Margaret. *Learning to Be Old: Gender, Culture, and Aging.* Lanham, Md.: Rowman and Littlefield, 2003.

Daniels, Magdalen. *Changing Woman's Workbook: Approaching Menopause as a Journey of Spiritual Transformation.* Los Angeles: Purple Iris Press, 1993.

Day, Alice Taylor. *Remarkable Survivors: Insights into Successful Aging among Women.* Washington, D.C.: Urban Institute Press, 1991.

Doress-Worters, Paula B., and Diana Laskin Siegal. *Ourselves, Growing Older: Women Aging with Knowledge and Power.* New York: Simon and Schuster, 1987.

Finger, Reta Halteman. "A New Wrinkle on Time: Women and Aging," *Daughters of Sara* 17 (1991).

Furman, Frida Kerner. "Women, Aging, and Ethics: Reflections on Bodily Experience," *The Annual of the Society of Christian Ethics* (1994).

Gannon, Linda. *Women and Aging: Transcending the Myths.* New York: Routledge, 1999.

Goudey, June Christine. *The Feast of Our Lives.* Cleveland: Pilgrim Press, 2002.

Heilbrun, Carolyn G. *The Last Gift of Time: Life beyond Sixty.* New York: Ballantine Books, 1998.

Hickman, Martha Whitmore. *Fullness of Time: Short Stories of Women and Aging.* Nashville: Abingdon Press, 1997.

Justes, Emma J. "Pastoral Care and Older Women's Secrets." In *Through the Eyes of Women: Insights for Pastoral Care.* Ed. Jeanne Stevenson Moesser. Minneapolis: Fortress Press, 1996.

Learn, Cheryl Demerath. *Older Women's Experience of Spirituality: Crafting the Quilt.* New York: Garland, 1996.

MacDonald, Barbara, and Cynthia Rich. *Look Me in the Eye: Old Women, Aging, and Ageism.* San Francisco: Spinsters Book Co., 1991.

Ramsey, Janet L., and Rosemary Blieszner. *Spiritual Resiliency in Older Women: Models of Strength for Challenges through the Life Span.* Thousand Oaks, Calif.: Sage, 1999.

Rosenthal, Evelyn R., ed. *Women, Aging, and Ageism.* New York: Haworth Press, 1990.

Shenk, Dena. "Honor Thy Mother: Aging Women in the Jewish Tradition." In *Aging and the Religious Dimension,* ed. L. Eugene Thomas. Westport, Conn.: Auburn House, 1994.

Thone, Ruth Raymond. *Women and Aging: Celebrating Ourselves.* New York: Harrington Park Press, 1992.

Walker, Margaret Urban. *Mother Time: Women, Aging, and Ethics.* Lanham, Md.: Rowman and Littlefield, 1999.

Resources on Religion and Aging

Anderson, Herbert, and Freda A. Gardner. *Living Alone.* Louisville: Westminster John Knox Press, 1997.

Becker, Arthur H. *Ministry with Older Persons: A Guide for Clergy and Congregations.* Minneapolis: Augsburg Publishing House, 1986.

Berrin, Susan, ed. *A Heart of Wisdom: Making the Jewish Journey from Midlife through the Elder Years.* Woodstock, Vt.: Jewish Lights Press, 1997.

Bianchi, Eugene C. *Aging as a Spiritual Journey.* New York: Crossroad, 1982.

Clements, William M. *Care and Counseling of the Aging.* Philadelphia: Fortress Press, 1983.

———. *Ministry with the Aging: Design, Challenges, Foundations.* New York: Harper and Row, 1981.

———. *Religion, Aging and Health: A Global Perspective.* New York: Haworth Press, 1989.

Clingan, Donald F. *Aging Persons in the Community of Faith: A Guide for Churches and Synogogues on Ministry with the Aging.* Indianapolis: Institute on Religion and the Indiana Commission on the Aging and Aged, 1980.

Coupland, Susan. *Beginning to Pray in Old Age.* Cambridge, Mass.: Cowley, 1985.

Everett, Deborah. *Forget Me Not: The Spiritual Care of Persons with Alzheimer's.* Edmonton, Alberta: Inkwell, 1996.

Fischer, Kathleen R. *Winter Grace: Spirituality for the Later Years.* New York: Paulist Press, 1985.

Harris, J. Gordon. *Biblical Perspectives on Aging: God and the Elderly.* Philadelphia: Fortress Press, 1987.

Hauerwas, Stanley, Carole Bailey Stoneking, Keith G. Meador, and David Cloutier. *Growing Old in Christ.* Grand Rapids, Mich.: Eerdmans, 2003.

Hendrickson, Michael C. *The Role of the Church in Aging.* New York: Haworth Press, 1986.

Hiltner, Seward, ed. *Toward a Theology of Aging.* New York: Human Sciences Press, 1975.

Hulme, William Edward. *Vintage Years: Growing Older with Meaning and Hope.* Philadelphia: Westminster Press, 1986.

Journal of Religion and Aging. New York: Haworth Press, 1984–present.

Journal of Religious Gerontology. New York: Haworth Press, 1990–present.

Kimble, Melvin A., and Susan H. McFadden. *Aging, Spirituality, and Religion: A Handbook.* Minneapolis: Fortress Press, 1995. Vol. 2, 2003.

Kirkland, Kevin H., and Howard McIlveen. *Full Circle: Spiritual Therapy for the Elderly.* Binghamton, N.Y.: Haworth Press, 1998.

Knutson, Lois D. *Understanding the Senior Adult: A Tool for Wholistic Ministry.* Bethesda, Md.: Alban Institute, 1999.

Koenig, Harold George. *Aging and God: Spiritual Pathways to Mental Health in Midlife and Later Years*. New York: Haworth Press, 1994.

Koenig, Harold George, Mona Smiley, and Jo Ann Ploch Gonzales. *Religion, Health, and Aging: A Review and Theoretical Integration*. Westport, Conn.: Greenwood Press, 1988.

Lammers, Stephen E., and Allen Verhey. *On Moral Medicine: Theological Perspectives in Medical Ethics*. Grand Rapids, Mich.: Eerdmans, 1987.

LeFevre, Carol, and Perry D. LeFevre. *Aging and the Human Spirit: A Reader in Religion and Gerontology*. 2nd ed. Chicago: Exploration Press, 1981.

Lester, Andrew D., and Judith L. Lester. *Understanding Aging Parents*. Philadelphia: Westminster Press, 1980.

Levin, Jeffrey S., ed. *Religion in Aging and Health: Theoretical Foundations and Methodological Frontiers*. Thousand Oaks, Calif.: Sage Press, 1994.

MacKinley, E. B. *The Spiritual Dimension of Aging*. London: Jessica Kingsley, 2001.

Maclay, Elise. *Green Winter: Celebrations of Later Life*. New York: Holt and Company, 1990.

Maldonado, D. "Hispanic and African American Elderly: Religiosity, Religious Participation, and Attitudes toward the Church," *Apuntes* 14, no. 1 (Spring 1994).

Maves, Paul B. *Faith for the Older Years: Making the Most of Life's Second Half*. Minneapolis: Augsburg Press, 1986.

McKim, Donald K., ed. *God Never Forgets: Faith, Hope, and Alzheimer's Disease*. Louisville: Westminster John Knox Press, 1997.

Missinne, Leo E. *Reflections on Aging: A Spiritual Guide*. Liguori, Mo.: Liguori, 1990.

Moberg, David O. *Aging and Spirituality: Spiritual Dimensions of Aging Theory, Research, Practice, and Policy*. New York: Haworth Press, 2001.

Morgan, Richard Lyon. *Fire in the Soul: A Prayer Book for the Later Years*. Nashville: Upper Room Books, 2000.

Nouwen, Henri J. M., and Walter J. Gaffney. *Aging: The Fulfillment of Life*. Garden City, N.Y.: Image Books, 1976.

Oliver, David B. *New Directions in Religion and Aging*. New York: Haworth Press, 1987.

Ram Dass. *Still Here: Embracing Aging, Changing, and Dying*. New York: Riverhead Books, 2000.

Sapp, Stephen. *Full of Years: Aging and the Elderly in the Bible and Today*. Nashville: Abingdon, 1987.

Schachter-Shalomi, Zalman, and Ronald S. Miller. *From Age-ing to Sage-ing: A Profound New Vision of Growing Older*. New York: Warner Books, 1995.

Seeber, James J. *Spiritual Maturity in the Later Years*. New York: Haworth Press, 1990.

Simmons, Henry C., and Jane Wilson. *Soulful Aging: Ministry through the Stages of Adulthood.* Macon, Ga.: Smyth & Helwys, 2001.

Stagg, Frank. *The Bible Speaks on Aging.* Nashville: Broadman Press, 1981.

Sullender, R. Scott. *Losses in Later Life: A New Way of Walking with God.* 2nd ed. New York: Haworth Press, 1999.

Thibault, Jane M. *A Deepening Love Affair: The Gift of God in Later Life.* Nashville: Upper Room, 1993.

Thomas, L. Eugene, and Susan A. Eisenhandler, eds. *Aging and the Religious Dimension.* Westport, Conn.: Auburn, 1994.

———. *Religion, Belief, and Spirituality in Later Life.* New York: Springer, 1999.

Vogel, Linda Jane. *The Religious Education of Older Adults.* Birmingham, Ala.: Religious Education Press, 1984.

Weaver, Andrew J., Harold George Koeniz, and Phyllis C. Roe, eds. *Reflections on Aging and Spiritual Growth.* Nashville: Abingdon Press, 1998.

Wicks, Robert J. *After Fifty: Spiritually Embracing Your Own Wisdom Years.* New York: Paulist Press, 1996.

For resources on aging in general, contact:

> The National Council on the Aging
> 300 D Street, SW, Suite 801
> Washington, DC 20024
> Phone: 202-479-1200
> *www.ncoa.org*

The music included in the book by Susan Ray Beehler can be found in the songbook *A Shared Journey.* For information about purchasing the songbook or accompanying CD, visit the website at *www.hacienda-springs.com,* or write to Hacienda Springs, Inc., 8103 La Paloma Circle, El Paso, TX 79907.

Notes

1. Henry C. Simmons, "Religious Education," in *Aging, Spirituality, and Religion,* ed. M. A. Kimble, S. H. McFadden, J. W. Ellor, and J. J. Seeber (Minneapolis: Augsburg Fortress, 1995), 227. Internal quotation by B. Meyerhoff, "Rites and Signs of Ripening: The Intertwining of Ritual, Time, and Growing Older," in *Age and Anthropological Theory,* ed. David I. Kertzer and Jennie Keith (Ithaca, N.Y.: Cornell University Press, 1984).

2. Maggie Wenig, "God Is a Woman and She Is Growing Older," sermon in *The Book of Women's Sermons,* ed. E. Lee Hancock (New York: Riverhead Books, 1999), 260.

3. Pierre Teilhard de Chardin, *Le Milieu Divin* (London: William Collins Sons, 1960), 89–90.

4. Census statistics for 2000 show that 12.4 percent of the total U.S. population, or 35 million people, are over sixty-five.

5. Historically the life of a human being was divided into three stages: childhood, adulthood, and old age. For women it was "maiden, mother, and crone." Today, however, people are living longer and staying active well into retirement. It is more common now to talk about the "four stages" or the "four quarters" of life, with aging constituting the fourth quarter.

6. William M. Clements, *Care and Counseling of the Aging* (Philadelphia: Fortress Press, 1979), 19–22, and Charles E. Curran, "Aging: A Theological Perspective," in *Aging and the Human Spirit: A Reader in Religion and Gerontology,* 2nd ed., ed. Carol LeFevre and Perry LeFevre (Chicago: Exploration Press, 1981), 74.

7. R. Scott Sullender, *Losses in Later Life* (New York: Haworth Pastoral Press, 1999), 42.

8. Ibid., 103.

9. U.S. Bureau of the Census, "Demographic and Socioeconomic Aspects of Aging in the United States," *Current Population Reports for 2000* (Washington, D.C.: U.S. Government Printing Office, 1984).

10. Robert O. Hansson, Jacqueline H. Remondet, and Marlene Galusha, "Old Age and Widowhood: Issues of Personal Control and Independence," in *Handbook of Bereavement: Theory, Research, and Intervention,* ed. Margaret S. Stroebe, Wolfgang Stroebe, and Robert O. Hansson (Cambridge: Cambridge University Press, 1993), 367.

11. Angela Berlis, *Psalm 71,* English translation Teresa Berger. Copyright © 2004. Used by permission of Angela Berlis and Teresa Berger. The (slightly longer) German original can be found in *Psalmen leben: Frauen aus allen Kontinenten lesen biblische Psalmen neu,* ed. Bärbel Fünfsinn and Carola

Kienel, Christlicher Glaube in der einen Welt 6 (Hamburg: EB-Verlag, 2002), 155–57.

12. James F. White, *Introduction to Christian Worship*, 3rd ed. (Nashville: Abingdon Press, 2003), 281.

13. Henry C. Simmons, "A Framework for Ministry for the Last Third of Life," in *Aging, Spirituality, and Religion*, vol. 2, ed. Melvin A. Kimble and Susan H. McFadden (Minneapolis: Fortress Press, 2003), 84.

14. White, *Introduction*, 280.

15. Ibid., 276.

16. "Service of Christian Marriage," *The United Methodist Hymnal* (Nashville: United Methodist Publishing House, 1989), 869.

17. This story was shared by a Presbyterian woman who was in a workshop I led in Texas more than a dozen years ago. I am sorry I do not remember her name, but her story has stayed with me to this day and has taken on a life of its own as I have passed it on to students. I am grateful to her for sharing this experience. It helped me when it was time for my own mother to relinquish her car keys. [LJV]

18. Dorothea McEwan, Pat Pinsent, Ianthe Pratt, and Veronica Seddon, eds., *Making Liturgy: Creating Rituals for Worship and Life* (Norwich, U.K.: Canterbury, 2001), 170–72; Dianne Neu, *Women's Rites: Feminist Liturgies for Life's Journey* (Cleveland: Pilgrim Press, 2003), 160–70; Rosemary Radford Ruether, *Women-Church* (San Francisco: Harper and Row, 1985), 204–6.

19. Lawrence Urdang, ed., *The Random House College Dictionary*, rev. ed. (New York: Random House, 1984), 318.

20. Susan Sontag, "The Double Standard of Aging," in *Psychology of Women: Selected Readings*, ed. J. S. Williams (New York: W. W. Norton, 1979), 478.

21. Stephen Sapp, "Ethics and Dementia: Dilemmas Encountered by Clergy and Chaplains," in *Aging, Spirituality, and Religion: A Handbook*, vol. 2, ed. Melvin A. Kimble and Susan H. McFadden (Minneapolis: Fortress Press, 2003), 357.

22. Published in "Reflections on Singing a New Song," Women's Division, General Board of Global Ministries, United Methodist Church, 2001. Translated into English by Jennifer Black Andrade.

23. From the musical "Jacques Brel Is Alive and Well and Living in Paris," music and French lyrics by Jacques Brel, English translation by Mort Shuman and Eric Blau.

24. Urban T. Holmes, "Worship and Aging: Memory and Repentance," in William M. Clements, *Ministry with the Aging* (San Francisco: Harper and Row, 1982), 94.

25. This liturgy was first published in Janet Walton, *Feminist Liturgy: A Matter of Justice* (Collegeville, Minn.: Liturgical Press, 2000), 68–70.

26. Each woman knew in advance which part of the body she would be blessing (arms, legs, eyes, ears, etc.). As each woman touched a particular part of Janet's body, they offered words that proclaimed that even though

she had lost her breasts, there were many other parts of her body that would enable her to live fully and responsibly in the world.

27. Dayle A. Friedman, "An Anchor amidst Anomie: Ritual and Aging," in *Aging, Spirituality, and Religion: A Handbook,* vol. 2, ed. Melvin A. Kimble and Susan H. McFadden (Minneapolis: Fortress Press, 2003), 141.

28. Holmes, "Worship and Aging: Memory and Repentance," 96–97.

29. Rabindranath Tagore, "Fireflies," in *Fireflies* (New York: Macmillan, 1965).

30. Ibid.

31. Martha Ann Kirk, CCVI, *Dancing with Creation: Mexican and Native American Dance in Christian Worship and Education* (Saratoga, Calif.: Resource Publications, 1983), 45.

32. Michael Joncas, "On Eagle's Wings," 1979 New Dawn Music, 1989 North American Liturgy Resources.

33. The inherent complexity and the colonization of Appalachian culture makes any claim about "tradition" overstated, but the following source offers sustained analysis in the field of Appalachian studies: Sandra L. Ballard and Patricia L. Hudson, eds., *Listen Here: Women Writing in Appalachia* (Lexington: University Press of Kentucky, 2003).

34. Arnold Van Gennep, *The Rites of Passage* (Chicago: University of Chicago Press, 1960).

35. Ronald Grimes, *Deeply into the Bone: Re-inventing Rites of Passage* (Berkeley: University of California Press, 2000), 5.

36. Ibid.

37. James K. Crissman, *Death and Dying in Central Appalachia: Changing Attitudes and Practices* (Urbana and Chicago: University of Illinois Press, 1994), 17.

38. Adapted from the *United Methodist Book of Worship* (Nashville: United Methodist Publishing House, 1992), 470–71.

39. Adapted from a Prayer of Thanksgiving found in the *United Methodist Book of Worship,* 150.

40. Anne Cameron, *Daughters of Copper Woman* (Vancouver, B.C.: Press Gang Publishers, 1981), 54.

41. Adapted from "The Legend of the Coming of Death," in Arthur C. Parker, *The Code of Handsome Lake, the Seneca Prophet*, 1913, as told to him by Edward Complanter in March 1906.

42. Written by Mary Elizabeth Mullino Moore for her mother's funeral service, June 2004.

43. A longer version of this essay appears in Teresa Berger, *Fragments of Real Presence* (New York: Crossroad, 2005).

44. Literally: "Remember, man, you are dust, and to dust you will return."

45. As trends do, the cultural avoidance of death has produced its own alarmed running commentary on this phenomenon as well as a number of countertrends. Among these countertrends are expanding forms of care at

the end of life, an interest in rituals of dying, and a growing scholarly interest in death studies across a variety of disciplines.

46. See, for example, Peter Gilmour, *Now and at the Hour of Our Death: Important Information Concerning My Medical Treatment, Finances, Death and Funeral,* rev. ed. (Chicago: Liturgy Training, 1999).

47. I would add to these a signed Organ Donation Card and a Declaration of Life, which affirms that if I should die as a result of violent crime, I would not wish the person found guilty to be subjected to the death penalty under any circumstances.

48. The contemplative practice of Music-Thanatology currently attempts to render present the power of music to the process of dying.

49. The full hymn text is available online in the Cyber Hymnal at *www.cyberhymnal.org.*

50. Francis of Assisi, "The Canticle of Brother Sun," in *Francis and Clare: The Complete Works,* trans. Regis J. Armstrong, Ignatius C. Brady, et al., The Classics of Western Spirituality (New York: Paulist, 1982), 39. It is unfortunate that the English translation uses the ambiguous term "man" when Francis's sentence clearly speaks about each and every "human being."

51. At least according to the Gospel of Luke (23:46).

52. Teresa Berger, *Fragments of Real Presence* (New York: Crossroad, 2005).

53. "A Statement of Faith of the United Church of Canada," *The United Methodist Hymnal* (Nashville: United Methodist Publishing House, 1989), 883.

Contributors

Rev. Dr. Susan Ray Beehler (United Methodist) is retired from the Piano faculty at the University of Texas, El Paso. Beehler is the co-composer and lyricist for the songs in the songbook *A Shared Journey* and composer for musicals and scripts for Hacienda Springs, Inc. Productions including "Clossetts," "The Party's Not Over," "Journey of Hope," and "Sistah! Sistah!"

Dr. Teresa Berger (Roman Catholic) is Professor of Theology at Duke Divinity School. Berger is the author and editor of several books, including *Women's Ways of Worship: Gender Analysis and Liturgical History* (Liturgical Press, 1999), *Dissident Daughters: Feminist Liturgies in Global Context* (Westminster John Knox Press, 2001), and *Fragments of Real Presence* (Crossroad, 2005).

Rev. Dr. Kathy Black (United Methodist) is the Gerald Kennedy Chair of Homiletics and Liturgics at the Claremont School of Theology. Black is the author of several books and articles, including *A Healing Homiletic: Preaching and Persons with Disabilities* (Abingdon, 1996), *Worship across Cultures: A Handbook* (Abingdon, 1998), and *Culturally-Conscious Worship* (Chalice, 2000).

Rev. Dr. Ruth Duck (United Church of Christ) is Professor of Liturgy at Garrett Evangelical Seminary. Duck is the author of several books and articles as well as a hymn writer. She has authored *Praising God: The Trinity in Christian Worship* with Patricia Wilson-Kastner (Westminster John Knox Press, 1999), *Finding Words for Worship* (Westminster John Knox Press, 1995), and *Circles of Care: Hymns and Songs* (Pilgrim Press, 1998).

Rev. Dr. Heather Murray Elkins (United Methodist) is Associate Professor of Homiletics and Liturgical Studies at Drew University. Elkins is the author of several books and articles, including *Worshiping Women: Reforming God's People for Praise* (Abingdon, 1994), *Pulpit, Table and Song: Essays in Celebration of Howard Hageman* (Scarecrow Press, 1995), *The Holy Stuff of Human Life* (Pilgrim Press, forthcoming), and "Tangible Evangelism" in *Preaching in the Context of Worship,* edited by David Greenhaw and Ronald Allen (Chalice, 2000).

Rev. Dr. Brigitte Enzner-Probst (German Lutheran) is a counselor at the Institute of Essential Counseling and a part-time chaplain at the Technical University in Munich, Germany. With Susan K. Roll and Annette Esser, Enzner-Probst is the editor of *Women, Ritual, and Liturgy,* European Society of Women in Theological Research Yearbook 9 (Peeters, 2001). She is the author of "The Role of the Body in the Liturgical Work of Women: Women Liturgies as Performances," in *Proceedings of the North American Academy of Liturgy,* 2004, and "Honoring the Wisdom of Old Women: Croning Rituals," in *Studia Liturgica* 32 (2002).

Martha Whitmore Hickman (United Methodist) is a writer of books for children and adults. Hickman is the author of *The Fullness of Time: Short Stories of Women and Aging* (Upper Room Books, 1990), *Such Good People* (Warner Books, 1996), and *Healing after Loss: Daily Meditations for Working through Grief* (HarperCollins Perennial, 1994).

Dr. Martha Ann Kirk, CCVI (Roman Catholic), is Professor of Religious Studies at University of the Incarnate Word in San Antonio, Texas. Kirk is the author of several books, including *Women of Bible Lands: A Pilgrimage to Compassion and Wisdom* (Liturgical Press, 2004), *Celebrations of Biblical Women's Stories: Tears, Milk, and Honey* (Sheed and Ward, 1987), and *Dancing with Creation* (Resource Publications, 1983).

Dr. Mary Elizabeth Mullino Moore (United Methodist) is Professor of Religion and Education and Director of Women in Theology and Ministry at the Candler School of Theology, Emory University. Moore is the author of several books and articles, including *Teaching as a Sacramental* Act (Pilgrim Press, 2004), *Sacramental Teaching* (Religious Education Press, 2000), *Ministry with the Earth* (Chalice, 1998), and *Teaching from the Heart* (Fortress Press, 1991).

Dr. Susan K. Roll (Roman Catholic) is Associate Professor in Theology at St. Paul University in Ottawa, Canada. Roll is the author of *Toward the Origins of Christmas* (Peeters, 1995). With Brigitte Enzner-Probst and Annette Esser she is the editor of *Women, Ritual and Liturgy,* European Society of Women in Theological Research Yearbook 9 (Peeters, 2001), and with Annette Esser and Anne Hunt Overzee she is the editor of *Re-Visioning Our Sources: Women's Spirituality in European Perspectives* (Peeters, 1997).

Dr. Deborah Sokolove (Christian) is the Curator of the Dadian Art Gallery at Wesley Theological Seminary in Washington, D.C.

Rev. Dr. Linda J. Vogel (United Methodist) is Professor Emerita of Christian Education and Senior Scholar at Garrett Evangelical Theological Seminary, Evanston, Illinois. Vogel is the author of several articles and books, including *Sacramental Living: Falling Stars and Coloring Outside the Lines* with Dwight W. Vogel (Upper Room Books, 1999), and *Syncopated Grace: Times and Seasons with God* (Upper Room Books, 2002). She is a contributor to *People of a Compassionate God: Creating Welcoming Congregations,* edited by Janet F. Fishburn (Abingdon, 2003).

Dr. Janet Walton (Roman Catholic) is Professor of Worship at Union Theological Seminary in New York. Walton is the author of several articles and books, including *Art and Worship: A Vital Connection* (Michael Glazier, 1988), *Women at Worship: Interpretations of North American Diversity,* with Marjorie Procter Smith (Westminster John Knox Press, 1993), and *Feminist Liturgy: A Matter of Justice* (Liturgical Press, 2000)